The *Strength* of My Soul

The *Strength* of My Soul

STORIES OF SISTERHOOD, TRIUMPH AND INSPIRATION

SharRon Jamison

THE STRENGTH OF MY SOUL
Published by The Jamison Group

Copyright © 2015 SharRon Jamison

ALL RIGHTS RESERVED.

No part of this book may be reproduced, distributed or transmitted in any form by any means, graphics, electronics, or mechanical, including photocopy, recording, taping, or by any information storage or retrieval system, without permission in writing from the publisher, except in the case of reprints in the context of reviews, quotes, or references.

All stories are the original writings of the credited authors. The publisher holds no responsibility for the accuracy or content of the individuals' stories.

Printed in the United States of America

ISBN (ebook): 978-1-942838-57-9

ISBN (paperback): 978-1-942838-56-2

Special discounts are available on bulk quantity purchases by book clubs, associations and special interest groups.
For details email: sharron@sharronjamison.com
or call (877) 296-4732.

Table of Contents

Acknowledgements	ix
Foreword	xi
Introduction	1

FAMILY TIES — 5

FRIEND OF THE DEVIL *Allie Greene*	7
THE COUCH WAS MY WITNESS *April VanMansfeld*	22
CIRCLE OF LOVE *Dr. Carole Hysmith*	38
MITOCHONDRIAL SEMANTICS *Michelle Dowell-Vest*	51
BECOMING...ME *Valerie Hall*	63

I MADE IT DESPITE THE ODDS — 79

IF I CAN, YOU CAN: DETERMINATION! *Anjelis Oliveira*	81

YOU ALMOST BROKE ME *Ava Cary*	94
SOME GIFTS COME IN UGLY WRAPPING PAPER *Dawn Westmoreland*	108
FACE IT, OR IT WILL FOLLOW YOU *SharRon Jamison*	122

LOVE AND LOSS — 131

ANCHORED IN LOVE *Brandy Jenkins and Nikki Rashan*	133
A BIG FISH AND A LITTLE RED BIRD *Nicole Varner*	143
SLEEPING WITH THE ENEMY *Denise Writer*	157

STORIES FROM MY WOMB — 173

STATISTICALLY SPEAKING *Angelia Henderson*	175
KEEP SHOWING UP FOR LOVE *Dr. Vikki Johnson*	189
BRAVE NEW MULES *Mimi Gonzalez*	198

I AM A CHILDLESS MOTHER *Valerie Chanell Jones*	205
"SEEING" THE FOREST FOR THE TREES *Yvette D. Bennett*	217

HEALTH AND HEALING	231

A PERCEIVED HURDLE IS NOT A HURDLE AT ALL *Colleen Pratt*	233
POWERFUL, POWERLESS, DIFFERENTLY EMPOWERED *Dr. Elaine Martin-Hunt*	244
ME, MOM AND DEMENTIA *Quentella Morris*	258
THE SUMMER OF CRAZY *Shannon Lagasse*	269
SLOWLY LOSING MOM *Sonia Ventura*	284

DEFYING CONVENTION	295

IS IT THE COLOR OF MY SKIN OR THE SCARF ON MY HEAD *Asila Abdul-Haqq*	297

MY GRANDPA'S POLITICS 307
Di Neo

MY UNFINISHED CHAPTER 321
Nijole Beth

LIVE LIFE ON YOUR OWN TERMS 335
Sheena Yap Chan

LIVING YOUR DREAMS 346
Kim J. King

Acknowledgements

To God, my Source of all good things, I am grateful to be used as your vessel.

To my son, Tariq Abdul-Haqq, sometimes you were my only reason to hold on. I love you!

To my parents, Rev. Franklin and Dorethia Jamison-Dixon, thank you for loving me and molding me. I hope that I am making you proud.

To Kim J. King, thank you for helping me during this process and supporting me in so many ways. You shared your expertise and resources so generously. Thank you. You are a blessing.

To Yvette D. Bennett, thank you for working so hard and embracing this project as your own. You were an angel sent from God. You were my right and left hand, my confidant, my cheerleader, and one of my biggest supporters. Thank you, Sis!

To Carrolle Moss, your support is unwavering. You are my gift and my Momma C. There are few people whom I can count on in life; you are one of those people. I love you.

The Strength of My Soul

To Marcella Austin, what a servant's heart! Thank you for being there for me and for always supporting me. I love you. And I am so grateful that I know that you love me, too.

To William Glenn Bean, you are a literary genius. Thank you for your direction, suggestions, and support. I am so grateful to serve in the ministry with you.

To Nicole Varner and Tiffany Hairston, thank you for always supporting me and lending your genius to every project. I celebrate you and Urban Bytes Photography.

To twenty-seven amazing women, thank you for opening up your life, your soul, and your spirits to contribute to this project! You gave from the deepest parts of your soul. Your words will bless, heal, and inspire women in ways that you will never know. I am so grateful to you! I honor and celebrate your talents and your time.

Thank you!

Foreword

By SharRon Jamison

Dear Sisters,

I believe in Sisterhood. Despite our differences in culture, class, education, age, race, faith, and sexual orientation, I believe that an indestructible tie binds us to each other's past experiences and forthcoming destinies. I believe that we are wonderfully linked and magnificently connected in mind, body, and spirit – that we are a sole (soul) tapestry that consists of all shapes and sizes, of distinct ideologies and preferences, and of unique shades and colors. We are a singular woven lattice of prolific lives that magnificently reflects the best of humanity.

My Sisters, you must believe that we are a sturdy people that can proudly claim and proclaim our messes and messages, our agonies and achievements, our fears and faith. Believe that the woman is a mighty, marvelous, and majestic creation. Believe that every woman is equipped and prepared to navigate and endure this amazing journey called LIFE!

The Strength of My Soul

My Sisters, I am prayerful that this profound collection of stories will align to inspire and encourage you. Know that the writers who contributed to this book unselfishly shared the dim crevices of their lives, bravely unlocking the chambers of their ailing hearts and courageously revealing the innermost sanctums of their souls with one unified hope: to encourage and enrich the lives of others, including you! I should forewarn you, though, that as you read and take this journey with me (with us), that you may experience many different, and sometimes contradicting, emotions – you may feel uncomfortable, angry, melancholy, confused, and even disgusted, so disgusted that you may question humanity and even yourself. This book may make you cry and cheer at the same time as you bear witness to the plight of *that woman* who endured unfair social conventions and a seemingly constant deluge of tragedy and despair.

Nonetheless, I am certain of a few things. As you read this tome of real-life stories, you will marvel at the strength of *that woman* who overcame insurmountable odds; you will marvel at your own reflection in *that woman* who sacrificed personal comforts for the good of others; you will celebrate *that woman* who defied the impossible for the sake of life, love, and liberation. Because *that woman* is you, and we are one. So as you read this book through the lenses of hope and acceptance, you will see you! You will see your struggles, your triumphs, and your own power. You will be reminded of your faith, your grace and, your unconquerable spirit. You will embrace your beauty, your boldness, and your blessings, and understand yourself differently as your gratitude for womanhood profoundly unfolds. So, I proclaim, with a high level of confidence and a great depth of assurance that we will be transformed!

You will be renewed!

You will be empowered!

You will be healed!

Finally, on behalf of every contributor to this collective witness, thank you for taking this sacred and righteous journey with us. We believe that we are you, that you are us, and that we are one. We believe that we are each other's keeper, and so it is with that belief that we fortify you with a love that lifts, a hope that heals, and a miracle that mends ... *so be blessed on this journey, my Sister.*

Be Blessed.

Introduction

I believe testimonies are one of our greatest sources of hope and inspiration. Stories of beating the odds, overcoming adversity, surviving tragedy, and defying the impossible are what motivates us; it is those very stories that keep us moving forward and onward in our lives. Sometimes, our own testimonies remind us of our inner strength, and sometimes the accounts of others awaken our belief in our greatness. Yet it is the stories, yours and mine, that affirm that we women are warriors and winners, full of promise, potential, and power.

The Strength of My Soul: Stories of Sisterhood, Triumph and Inspiration is a reading experience that exemplifies an important healing principle: you must reveal to heal. And even though every author had a different experience and healing process, they have all exposed secrets that shamed them, pain that poisoned them, circumstances that nearly claimed them, grief that almost paralyzed them, or a perspective that elevated them. All of the authors shared, cried, strategized, and some even relived their painful experiences to help you and others as you travel on your own healing and life journeys. They revealed so that women could be healed.

Despite their confessions and revelations, the authors didn't provide promises or solutions, because we all know there is no handbook on how to deal with the vicissitudes of life; we learn as we go. However, I believe that every triumph and every challenge creates opportunities for us to grow and learn. I believe that every connection with women, the sisterhood, offers a space to heal our souls, repair our broken wings, and mend our broken hearts. I believe it is within the safety of the sacred community of other women, our soul sisters, that we remove the shackles of our past in order to soar into the potential of our future. Our communion and our willingness to engage in community are what fortify our collective souls.

The Strength of My Soul is not a "how-to" book, nor is it a book of that endorses victimhood. It is a collection that hopefully shakes you and shifts you to think, live, and love differently so that you can arrive at a place of peace, power, and self-love.

It is a literary feast that helps you realize the best in yourself and pushes you into your destiny.

SharRon Jamison

You may find it helpful to read each story with a journal and pen nearby so you can capture your most authentic thoughts and feelings. If you can, please don't discount your initial reaction or instinct, because many times what first resonates in our spirit is often where our truth lies.

Thank you for sharing this wonderful journey with us. We applaud you, and we celebrate the strength of your soul!

Blessing to you always,

SharRon Jamison

Family Ties

FRIEND OF THE DEVIL

Allie Greene

I celebrated my thirteenth birthday in a locked ward of a juvenile psychiatric facility. I was not suicidal, psychotic, or neurotic, nor was I addicted to any drugs or alcohol. I had not tortured any animals or people, or run away from home (all reasons the other juveniles had been admitted for). I was at a loss. Why was I locked up, surrounded by stuffed animals and birthday balloons?

With any story, you sometimes have to revisit the beginning to understand how or why you got where you are. It has been difficult to crawl back through the shadowy tunnel of my chaotic childhood memories to find peace with certain events. Many of my caregivers were completely dysfunctional, and some were even abusive. I have told my story many times from the safety of my intellect, accepting that it is my life. Trying to heal from it, however, has been a completely different experience.

I was born in New York City to a young mother and an older, bigamist father. They were married, and my mom left him when I was just over a year old, after discovering his first wife and three kids tucked away in another part of the city. In those early years, my mother did her best to raise me. She managed to provide for my basic needs, but she never seemed to enjoy being a mother. I felt like I was never her top priority, and she pawned me off on others, including my grandmothers and aunt, to give herself a break. She was frequently stricken with some illness or injury, and we often wound up living with her boyfriends, friends, or families from our various churches. However, what she lacked in stability, she made up for in personality. At times, my mother was loveable, larger than life, artistic, and silly.

At an early age, I assumed the role of the mother and she the child, and we are still playing those roles today. My mom struggled with alcoholism and addiction, and masked her inability to function properly by immersing herself in religion. We moved around a lot between Massachusetts and

Allie Green

New York, but she always found a church to dictate our daily routine and church elders to guide her life decisions. She gravitated toward conservative, fundamentalist churches that bordered on cult-like indoctrination, which is why I still struggle with my religious beliefs today. I often felt she hid behind religion to avoid being held accountable for her actions or decisions. The combination of her non-parenting skills and her unconventional parenting style made for an unpredictable, sometimes fun and wild, early childhood. Despite all this, I was a good student, made friends easily wherever we wound up, and was slightly mischievous.

I started sixth grade in a new school in Massachusetts. Halfway through the year, I was sent to live with my aunt and uncle in North Carolina. My mother was going to New York to stay with my grandmother while attempting sobriety. Moving around so much was unsettling. Yet, for as much anger and resentment that I had toward my mother, I was always very protective of her. The summer before seventh grade, she moved to North Carolina, full of hope for the future with a six-month AA chip in hand. Later, I would blame the car accident that occurred a few months after the move as the catalyst for the life of turmoil that ensued. Eventually, I realized it was a combination of factors waiting for the perfect storm.

My childhood descended further down a dark rabbit hole after my mother's accident. She suffered a closed head injury characterized by continual brain swelling that affected neurological pathways integral for the body to function. Her decline happened gradually. First, my mother lost her ability to walk and speak clearly. She also lost her ability to make simple, ordinary decisions and to process information. Slowly, the little bit of mother I had left disappeared, and the effects of the accident left her living in a full-time rehabilitation facility for almost three years, relearning basic motor and cognitive skills and daily activities that most of us take for granted. During this time, I was horrified, terrified, and confused. The trauma of my mom's head injury resulted in extreme behaviors and memory loss. She easily became overwhelmed in noisy, crowded places, and she experienced complete sensory overload on top of debilitating paranoia. She didn't remember chunks of my childhood or key life events. She lost her ability to make rational decisions, often resulting in destructive choices and behavior.

It was ultimately my mother's inability to function,

not my own misbehavior, that landed me in the juvenile psychiatric ward of the county hospital where I would turn thirteen. My mom had dropped me off at the hospital one evening a few days after I had snuck out of the house one night. Who knew those childish actions would forever shape my life? Hospital staff eventually disclosed that I was admitted for demonstrating "out-of-control" behavior, and it was years before I realized the definition of "out of control" had various meanings for different people. To my mother, defending myself against her assaulting rage was "out of control." This incident happened after she had overheard me making plans to sneak out of our house with my girlfriends one night, shortly after the accident had occurred. One of her many symptoms was slipping into comatose-like sleep cycles that could last up to sixteen hours. I had begun to take advantage of these episodes and started to regularly sneak out of the house for most of the summer, arriving home before dawn.

After listening in on the phone conversation, my mother had stormed into my room, beat me with the buckle side of a belt, and alerted all my friend's parents about their daughters' plans. Overnight, I became the most hated girl at my middle school. Kids labeled me a "snitch" and their parents "a ring leader" (because there was no way these affluent Happy Valley kids would have snuck out without my influence). I was accused of being "jealous" because I didn't have a boyfriend. Some classmates even surmised that my supposed "snitching" was my way of getting back at everyone that did. Since I was different and had lived in the area for only a few months, I was an easy scapegoat. Overnight I had lost friends that I had made less than a year earlier.

I had already felt like an outsider because I was the new, brown girl from up North who had moved to a mostly White, upper-class neighborhood. My mother is White and my dad is Spanish and Native American, which wasn't common in the South and automatically made the kids ask "if my Daddy was Black." We lived in a lovely, two-bedroom apartment in a new development with a pool, not a big, fancy house on the golf course like the majority of the students who attended my school. My mom was also not like the stay-at-home moms in the neighborhood; she worked full time, including some evenings, at a car dealership, and we had no kin or ties to the community. To make matters worse, I rode the school bus and our apartment complex was the last stop before school. Other buses and students in cars en route to school passed by and knew where I lived, frequently commenting on this. No one of any clout rode the bus. Riding the bus was for Blacks and rednecks, not affluent, country club Whites.

Ultimately, the other girls caught sneaking out were grounded for the remainder of the summer. I was the lucky one who was committed to a psychiatric ward. Of course, my punishment clearly did not fit the crime. Ironically, the hospital turned out to be one of the most peaceful places I had been in some time. It also began the trend of institutional settings I would be sent to in the coming years. In fact, the "psych ward" wasn't that bad at all. The staff was nice and dependable, and we had a routine, something I had lacked in my own house, with regularly scheduled meal times, activities, TV viewing, and nap time!

After completing mandatory therapy sessions, I earned visitation privileges and day passes to leave the ward. These were fun days, even though the only visitors I had were my aunt and uncle. I had authority over my visitation list and kept my mother off of it. My mother's health was diminishing, so I am not sure she noticed. For one of the first times ever, I felt like someone was listening to me, and that I actually had some control over my topsy-turvy life. Eventually, I even earned a double-occupancy room for my "good behavior." I decorated the walls with collages I made from torn pages of magazines, mostly photographs of Beautiful perfume and Guess jeans ads with Claudia Schiffer in them, which I had stolen from the Community Room. I was also allowed to have my comforter, sheets, and stuffed animals brought from home. Soon, I settled right in. I felt, safe, secure, and relatively happy, which were foreign feelings to me. In reality, I had been there almost two months. No one was really sure why, and I think the staff had taken pity on me.

My mother's condition deteriorated, and doctors recommended she be placed indeterminately in a full-time care facility that specialized in neurological disorders and head trauma. My aunt and uncle were willing to become my legal guardians, but unbeknownst to us all, my mother had consulted with church friends in New York and had made arrangements to send me to boarding school. It may have been another sign of her impaired thinking, but she never considered letting me stay with them, nor did she discuss her decision with me, and I was furious! After two long drives with my aunt and uncle between North Carolina and Pennsylvania, which included several interviews (a few failed, one nailed), I was awarded a full scholarship. Arrangements were made for me to go directly from one institutional setting to another.

My time in boarding school is another chapter for a different book. In the three years I was there I experienced a motley assortment of emotions and adventures. I was scared, and I felt abandoned, displaced, and unloved. I was worried about everything from my mom's health to my own well being, while trying to adjust to yet another state and another new school. The campus was on a working dairy farm, and we lived in houses clustered together with a set of house parents and ten to sixteen students in each home. We functioned like family units with weekly chores, including cooking, cleaning, and barn duty. I had more structure and routine than I had ever known. Sometimes I rebelled, because I didn't know how else to cope or because I wanted to keep things interesting. One of my biggest challenges was interpreting the social/cultural nuances of living every hour of every day with my classmates. In the end, we shared a coming-of-age journey that included laughter, tears, and deep friendships that continue to sustain me.

Despite the difficult adjustment, I excelled academically and was chosen to take a course at Penn State University the summer after tenth grade. When the program ended, I would spend a week with my mother. She was back in North Carolina, recently released from the hospital. While visiting, she began dangling carrots of "a more traditional high school experience." It wasn't hard to tempt me, because I wanted a mother and to have a semblance of normalcy in my completely abnormal life. So, I started my eleventh school as a high school. Junior. Little did I know that that decision would haunt me for years.

Moving back to North Carolina, and in with my mother, was one of the worst decisions of my life. If only I had known then. My mom had joined a Pentecostal church and convinced she'd received a gift in which she could hear directly from God. She also claimed demons were plaguing our house in the form of insects and moths. At times, she walked from room to room, swinging a broom, speaking in Tongues, and casting spirits out of our home. Yes, this was strange behavior, but I loved and felt protective of her and dealt with it the best I could. Later, I understood that these were textbook symptoms of paranoid schizophrenia.

Soon, my life became a living hell. Delusional, she accused me of being the "Devil's disciple and spawn," and seemed determined to beat him out of me. I endured belt beatings, punishments, and groundings for minor, imagined offenses. Dragging me to Christian functions became another form of punishment. I eventually discovered, through family snooping, that many of my "offenses" were things my mother had been accused of when she was a child.

Right before Thanksgiving, my mother kicked me out of the house. I was defending myself against one of her habitual beatings and had tried to hit her back. (This was eerily similar to the situation that led her to commit me to the county hospital when I was twelve.) I tried to return to boarding school; however, my mother had removed me without going through the proper channels and, consequently, I was ineligible to return. With nowhere else to go, I stayed in North Carolina and moved in with my aunt and uncle. They are kind-hearted, loving people who did their best to help a troubled teenager. Nevertheless, once again, I felt displaced and unloved, with no control over my life. I was sad and frustrated as I watched them interact with their young son, keenly aware that I would never have parents who could love and provide for me the way they did for him. I had a case of cousin rivalry that would have put siblings to shame.

By the fall of my senior year, I was so uncomfortable that I decided to move out of my aunt and uncle's home. The decision to leave seemed easy, because I was already contributing to my own financial support, and since I worked two jobs, I felt more like an adult than a child. Petrified, I moved in with a couple I had met through work and paid them $100 rent a month, including groceries and utilities. A condition of my living with them was that I had to graduate from high school and attend college. I considered emancipation, but I decided against it since I would turn eighteen that summer. As a minor without legal guardians, I quickly learned how to forge my mother's signature. Through sheer determination, I managed to graduate from high school and was accepted into college.

My mother never fully recovered from her accident. She continued to make poor decisions, including four sometimes-abusive marriages, and had more home addresses than I can remember.

Allie Green

At one point, she ended up in jail because she could neither remember nor prove who she was. When I was twenty-seven years old, she finally admitted her paranoid schizophrenia diagnosis to me. After researching the illness, I realized that the behavior I had witnessed growing up was symptomatic of the disease. I was both saddened and relieved to finally have an explanation for her bizarre and abusive behavior. Today, she is unable to work, and after receiving a small compensation for the accident, has been dependent on government benefits for most of her life. She is currently in a loving, long-term relationship and, surprisingly, she has not remarried.

My mother and I are not close, and we do not have much of a relationship. Thinking of her upsets me, and I have a lot of unresolved anger towards her and my childhood. I'm angry with her for abandoning me and for failing to be the mother I wanted or needed, and those feelings are also accompanied by guilt for harboring anger toward someone who is clearly both mentally and physically ill. I still struggle with some of those dark memories and with discerning the symptoms of her head injury from her undiagnosed mental illness. Striving to love and understand someone who is sick while trying to recover from so much of my own pain and loss has been a tough balancing act.

My healing and validation has come in many forms. Dear friends have become my surrogate family, and I have a nationwide support network that I work hard to upkeep. I keep in touch with my family and many of the folks who have helped me along this journey. The gift of all this chaos is that, as an adult, I have learned how to forge healthier relationships. Through all the ups and downs, often with only myself to depend on, I never gave up. I clawed my way out of the rabbit hole.

I am not at the finish line yet, since this is truly a marathon and not a sprint, but I am really close.

Allie Greene graduated from the University of North Carolina at Chapel Hill with a Bachelors of Arts in Studio Art. She currently lives in Los Angeles, California, and has been working in feature film production for over ten years. With a love of photography, travel, foreign places, and cultures, she intends to visit all seven continents in her lifetime. After completing Pilates instructor training in 2014, she is eagerly drafting the next chapter of her life.

THE COUCH WAS MY WITNESS

April VanMansfeld

I remember sitting on the couch. It was a beige, leather couch that swallowed you like a grandma's hug and held you close while you peeled back the layers of your soul. The couch heard every muffled sob. Every curse. Every secret. Every rant. Every epiphany. Every laugh, first sardonic, then deprecating, and finally joyous. She held me up as I told my truth and discovered all the nooks and crannies I'd used to survive my childhood. The couch was my confidant. She bore witness to my metamorphosis.

This time, I'd come to therapy because my relationship was crashing and burning and I didn't know how to fix it. I knew my needs weren't being met, and I knew my partner wasn't happy either. The more I tried to make the relationship work, the worse things got. Not only was my relationship in peril, but I had a tween who suffered from chronic migraines and irritable bowel syndrome that necessitated a flexible schedule so I could both care for her while keeping the family financially afloat. Because of this, as a self-employed single parent, I felt overwhelmed and stretched beyond my means in every aspect of my life.

For months I anchored on the couch and rattled and rambled about my epic failures. I failed to finish my college degree. I failed to stay in relationships. I failed as a mother since we were poorer than hell and all I had managed to teach her was how to survive. I failed as a friend, too preoccupied with paying rent and utilities to really be there for those who always managed to show up for me. Everything I started, I failed to complete.

I will always be grateful to my therapist, Kristine, for prying open my self-loathing and helping me speak my pain and inadequacies aloud. She let me spew for months about my shortcomings, and then she shifted my focus to healing. During one session, as I pressed deeper into the comfort and safety of the beige couch, Kristine asked if I was open to looking at my birth order and considering how much influence it may have had on my life choices and patterns. It was the first good gut laugh I'd had in three months. I explained to her that I was my mother's only child, my father's oldest, and my stepfather's youngest, and that in chronological order, my older brother and I were the middle children. Only. Oldest. Youngest. Middle. All at the same time.

When I looked up, Kristine's facial expression was a mix of perplexed awe and steely resolve. Kristine shut the book on her birth order theory, smiled, and told me my clarification "explained so much." My birth order gave her some much-needed insight into areas that needed deeper work. That turned out to be an understatement along the lines of referring to childbirth as "slightly uncomfortable." I refer to those early therapy years as the Years of Leaping. Deep breaths. Baby steps. And leaping.

I'd spent years thinking I was deeply in touch with my emotions, only to have Kristine help me distinguish between actually knowing how I felt and my habit of answering "feeling" questions with "doing" answers. She literally had to pull out a chart with facial expressions matched with words underneath, asking me to point to the one that most matched how I felt about certain subjects. We spent years working on learning to actually say what I wanted out loud. It would be years later before I learned to add "in front of others," "when asked," "in spite of fearing ridicule or misunderstanding," and "before I was livid and demanding instead of requesting" to that process. As we dug deeper into my wounded areas, Kristine introduced me to re-visioning, and with that success, emotionally focused therapy, or EFT. For pre-verbal rage, we found that beating a pillow with a whiffle ball bat while giving voice to the pain worked wonders. It's not that everything got fixed; it's that we did the work of finding therapeutic tools that I continue to use as I navigate life.

Soon, I realized that my deepest wounds, my negative self-talk, and all of the deep, abysmal pain were byproducts of having three narcissistic parents. My feelings of anguish, loneliness, despair, betrayal, and rage were the gifts of parents who could not or would not fully love me. My invisible scars were from the negligence of a father who abandoned me and from the mother who refused to parent me but had the capacity to co-parent another child. My emotional scabs were from a stepfather who loved me, but only as an appendage of my mother, never for myself.

The wounds from my birth father were preverbal and invasive. Even though he never lived more than twenty minutes away, I rarely saw him. When he did call to schedule a visit, I was not guaranteed to see him on time or to see him at all. Sometimes I would wait for hours, not eating or playing, just sitting, hoping that he would pull into the driveway. My father's inability to show up affected not only our relationship, but also the relationships that I could not fully develop with the paternal side of my family. The pain was deep, and I grew up without the ability to fully verbalize or even see how deep those wounds were. His failure to make me a priority showed up in almost every area of my life.

Mama's abandonment was different. She was never very affectionate, but I'd gotten used to sporadic hugs and occasional praise. Early on, I felt that I was an extension of her, and that I was to always do my best to reflect what she wanted to see. When I was five, I went to live with my mother's parents while she moved in with my future stepfather and his son. It was a temporary arrangement that lasted for three years. I visited her every other weekend or so, and I spoke with her on the phone when I didn't visit. Even though my daily care was left to my grandmother, my mother was still in my life.

I don't know when I became aware of it, but I remember hearing my soon-to-be older brother calling my mother "mom" years before I transitioned from calling his father Mr. Gerry. I remember thinking, "Why was this boy, who wasn't my brother, calling my mother mom? Why was it okay for her, my mother, to live with and take care of this other man's child instead of staying with me to mother me?" Even after my mother finally came to get me for good and she married my stepfather, I still referred to the man who housed, clothed, and fed me as Mr. Gerry instead of "dad" for another year.

I felt like an outsider, an inconvenient afterthought. The three of them all had the same last name and knew their place in their unit. My main focus became to prove to my mother and her now husband that they hadn't made a mistake in bringing me into their home, that I was worthy of their effort to provide for me. So, at ten, I converted to Catholicism, and at twelve, I agreed to being adopted. Basically, I spent all of my teen years both trying to earn approval and love *and* remain invisible. I became very good at making sure they had no reason to complain about my chores or schoolwork. I hustled and saved my allowance so I could contribute to, and later fully pay for, holiday gifts for family and friends. I saved for my yearly back-to-school shopping. I asked for as little as possible, using my own funds to pay for outings with friends or club dues for school organizations. On the rare occasions I asked my parents for money, I had my elevator speech ready, my list of all the things I'd done to justify their out-of-pocket assistance to cover costs for some school or extracurricular activity, or to drive me somewhere out of their normal routine. I showed them who they wanted to see, the side that most closely meshed with what they wanted and needed, while my true self lived for the moments spent with friends whose true selves were equally invisible in their homes. By keeping my parents happy and not giving them any reason to closely examine what was really going on with me, I was able to build a family of misfits that accepted, nurtured, and supported each other in ways our families of origin could not.

What a mess. What started as an attempt to fit into the family became a mask to wear to protect myself just in case they could not accept me or want me because I wasn't neat or smart or "good." In my young mind's eye, they would have never left me behind if I'd had any hope of being the little girl they *really* wanted. For all intents and purposes, my parents provided a wonderful suburban middle class life for me, and I played the role of dutiful daughter until graduation, unknowingly taking the mask with me into my adult life.

I spent my childhood, actually most of my life, feeling as if I were too much and not enough for either of my parents. I was too much responsibility for my father, yet not loveable enough to compel him to parent me. I was too much for my mother to shoulder the burden of raising me on her own, yet not loveable enough for her to give up the lifestyle she envisioned for herself. I was too much responsibility and expense for my stepfather, even though my mother was co-parenting his child. And I was not loveable enough for him to make permanent space for me before marrying my mother so we could become a family together. I was too much and not enough. Only. Oldest. Youngest. Middle.

Time curled up on the beloved couch and made sense of the bits and pieces of my trifold imprinting. It painted a picture of me growing from childhood into adulthood with a strong sense of having to either entertain anyone who paid the slightest bit of attention to me, or having to care for every need of whoever acted as if he or she wanted to be in my life. I never truly trusted that people really wanted to know my true self, or that they would stay long enough to get to know me. I played this scenario out in my life repeatedly by consistently picking lovers on the narcissism spectrum.

The ache for unconditional love and subsequent deep wounding due to the absence of love was the fuel that kept me moving forward when my basic non-material needs weren't being met. That inner two-, five-, eight-, and eleven-year-old me that seethed with rage at being unseen, unheard, unwanted, and unknown. I often felt like an afterthought, and as an adult, I vowed to never let myself feel that way.

I spent most of my adult life angry with and resentful of my parents for all the ways they failed to show up and love me. Time on the couch, hugged up and loved on in her comfort, as well as a desire to be my best self while I was still young enough to enjoy it, meant doing some hard work to see my life and myself in new ways. Investing time and money in me shifted my view of my life and myself.

Today, I have an amazing relationship with my now grown daughter, disproving my theory that I'm not good with long-term commitment or nurturing love. Six years, a few raises, and a promotion in the same career with the same company disprove my theory I couldn't stay or grow with a company for secure, stable income. Friends from elementary school, high school, and early college years who are affirming, challenging, and uplifting, remind me that I *do* know how to pick loving, beautiful spirits to be in relationship with, and that platonic familial love matters. A closer relationship with my younger sister and brothers reminds me that I am most definitely our father's daughter, and that some of his traits, habits, and preferences come hardwired in me as I share them with the same people who share my DNA but weren't raised with me.

By doing the work nestled on the couch, I freed myself to make space for my parents so I could hold them in different lights and from different angles. Now I see them as scared kids and as adults with hopes, dreams, and plans. I can see that they tried to figure out their new job titles of "parent" and "spouse." They made mistakes and missteps without the benefit of peripheral or backward views. The benefit of my couch-time was remembering, owning, and forgiving. Today, I am grateful.

Through all of this, I forgave the father that raised me for his humanness, albeit twenty years after his death. I also showed up at the hospital in mid-July, 2014, when my sister called and said our father was in the ICU with stage 4 lung cancer. She said due to his COPD and blood pressure, he might not live long enough to receive treatment. That decision to go to the hospital allowed him to see the four of us love, laugh, tease, and embrace as siblings in ways he had not witnessed in more than thirty years. It also allowed me to visit him several times on my own while he recovered enough to go home and then show up again a month later as his health took a turn for the worse. By letting go of the need to be right, to be vindicated, I was able to be alone with my father for hours the last time he was admitted to the hospital. I was able to say things to him that I'd never said and would never get to say again.

In spite of its toxic craziness, the time on the couch helped me forge a better relationship with my mother. Her diagnosis with inoperable stage-four lung cancer in June 2014 led to my decision to rearrange my work schedule and home life to be with her through her treatment and long days of bed rest. The turn in our interactions these past months have given me more depth, closure, joy, and healing than I ever thought possible.

The benefit of time spent curled on the couch hugging myself, re-parenting, and growing me is recognizing that all of my experiences went into shaping my personhood, my perspective, and my very existence. Allowing my parents to be as fully human, complicated, flawed, and loveable as they really were allows me to be fully human, complicated, flawed, and loveable, too. Because of the time I spent on the couch and the subsequent work that I continue to do, I am more deeply and profoundly in love with myself. I no longer feel the need to martyr myself or abandon my needs to appear easier or more worthy of love.

I may never finish my degree. I may never publish even one of the five cookbooks swirling around my head. I may never have a lover who is a soul mate or a life partner who'll meander along with me for the rest of my life. And that's fine! I learned to stop setting goals to "show" folks that I am worthy. Now, when I set and achieve the goals that make my heart sing, the why and how will evolve around my heart's desires and my spirit's calls to share the gifts the divine has given me. My goals will not become some twisted need to prove anything to anyone other than my highest self.

My year spent living with rural indigenous populations, recording recipes and folklore and working it into my own cooking lexicon, will be for *me*. My bath and body products, soothing and nurturing the bodies of hardworking folks, will be for *me*. My bed and breakfast, displaying and selling local art, pottery, furnishings, my body products, and those five cookbooks, will be for *me*. I am embracing the radically ridiculous notion that I am not too much or not enough for all the spaces, places, and lives that are meant to intersect with me. No, if anything, I am exactly who, where, and with whom I'm meant to be. I am satisfied in ways only the divine needs to know. I am just right and perfectly made, and the albatross of unworthiness no longer weighs me down. I am on that precipice, taking the leap and soaring for the joy of it. I am landing firmly, gently on my own two feet.

And the couch? She is there in all her glory, ever ready to hold my secrets and my heart as I do the work of excavating myself.

April VanMansfeld
Entrepreneur, underwriter, author

A native of Atlanta, April resides in the city's historic WestLake/Mozley Park area with her daughter and fur babies. She is humbled and proud to have taken on the task of owning and renovating the nearly eighty-year old home her grandfather built for her grandmother. April is a proud and loud advocate for middle-class African Americans stepping up to the challenges of re-gentrifying historically black communities and proudly becoming the new faces of urban pioneering. To that end, she smiles a little deeper each time she's questioned about her love of gardening, her desire to raise chickens, her longing for pygmy goats, and how that fits in a community barely two miles from the heart of downtown Atlanta. That's when she knows she's not speaking with a generational native; natives know just how well the old communities can sustain an urban farmer.

The Strength of My Soul

After more than twenty years in the corporate arena, and over a decade of owning her own business services company, TigerWolf, Inc., April is very proud to be a life and disability underwriter for one of the largest insurance providers in the country. She sees her job as not only a beautiful homage to her love of sociology and statistics, but also a lifelong commitment to social justice and community work as well. Helping small companies provide resources for their employees at critical moments has become its own reward. April looks forward to the very near future when she can return to her alma mater, Agnes Scott College, and finish her Bachelors of Science in Sociology and later pursue her masters. She's contemplating another bachelors degree in culinary arts, since ultimately plans to run a bed and breakfast in the metro area serving up the dishes her friends, family, and clients regularly request.

While she has been in and out of the local open mic/poetry scene for the past fifteen years, it's her cookbooks that keep those who know of them requesting a publishing date. Within the next year, April hopes to publish the first in a series of five. She will also be a contributor in a yet untitled anthology spearheaded by the unconquerable Claudia Moss. She is still in a state of shock to be

April VanMansfeld

included in such an incredible collaboration with the diverse and inspiring group of women contributing to this compilation.

THE CIRCLE OF LOVE

Dr. Carole Hysmith

The Union between a Mother and Her Same-Gender Loving Daughter

"All that the Father gives Me will come to Me, and the one who comes to me I will certainly not cast out." - John 6:37

I have been blessed with giving birth to two children, one who is a same-gender loving woman and the other my son, whose unexpected life challengers awakened the latent genes of his father's family history of mental illness. In order to encourage you in this brief chapter to move out of your own way, I will only elaborate on my experiences with my daughter, who rocked my world when I discovered she was a lesbian. Over thirty years later, I have realized that knowing this about her has enriched my character and our relationship. My son's mental challenges and the circle of his mother's love will be discussed in my forthcoming book, *Moving Out of Our Own Way: Seven Lessons to Spiritually Live Your Life with Zeal*.

Moving out of my own way was quite a challenge. My tumultuous life-canvas includes the portrait of a sexually abused child at ten years old, an unwed mother at fifteen, a high school dropout at eighteen, a married woman at nineteen, an abused mother of two at twenty-five, a bereaved mother who mourned the loss of her unborn third child at thirty-three, a cancer survivor at thirty-four, a divorcee at thirty-eight, and a grandmother of a physically challenged child at forty-two. Seven years later, on Saturday May 2, 1987, I became another national statistic by getting married for the second time. Today, I am still in that relationship.

The Circle of Love: A Mother's View

My daughter, Myishia, my first-born, expressed her love for me by innocently embracing me as her friend and confidant. Myishia can be described as a "free spirit" who got the short end of the stick because I was so young when she was born. As a young mother at fifteen, still in high school, I kept my secret of being pregnant for the full nine months. If anyone noticed my weight gain or my belly, neither my mother nor my siblings mentioned it. Consequently, when my father, who did not live with us, came to visit while I was in the hospital, he became beside himself during our discussion. My father was an intelligent, compassionate man of discernment, but during that traumatic time in my family's life, his anger preceded his logic and compassion. Ultimately, he gave me "food for thought" through a healthy discussion on the gift of "free choice" and the consequences of our decisions.

My father persuaded me to either give my baby up for adoption or place her in a foster home so I could finish school. I later discovered that when my father learned of the statuary rape of his virgin fifteen-year-old middle child by a twenty-two-year-old man, he was livid and made various attempts to take legal action through the court system to no avail. In retrospect, I believe my father felt violated, devalued, and disrespected as a man and as a father. However, with time, he was able to move out of his own way.

Dr. Carole Hysmith

After much soul searching and discernment, due to the finality clauses in legal documents, I chose not to give my daughter up for adoption. Instead, I chose to put her in a foster home. Since I was still in high school, I placed Myishia for one year in a Catholic adoption agency called The Angel Guardian Home for Little Children located in the Bay Ridge area of Brooklyn, New York. During her confinement, I was not able to bring her home, but I could stay connected with her through periodic visits on my own. By God's good grace, this adoption agency also took care of their resident's foster care placements. Thus, Myishia was fortunate enough to be placed in a foster home in St. Albans, New York, until the age of three. During that time, since I was able to bring Myishia home with me almost weekly, my life as a woman and mother solidified. Because I was so young, I constantly evaluated my neophyte motherly instincts. Sometimes it was difficult to travel from my house to the foster home where she stayed, but I always made the effort. Since no one in my family had a car, I either traveled for more than an hour by subway or a neighbor would supportively drive me. Apparently, my visits to Myishia and the bond we created were of great value to her. Looking back, I'm glad I moved out of my own way and made those visits.

My plan was to bring Myishia home after I graduated from high school. Unfortunately, I did not graduate with my class because I failed history. Consequently, another significant and life- changing choice had to be made! I chose to drop out of high school to independently care for my three-year old daughter.

Unlike many mother-daughter teenage relationships, Myishia unequivocally trusted me. This level of trust was established because of our open communication and my candidness with her as we both matured. This channel of communication was a conscious choice on my part, since my greatest fear was that the outside world would inform her about her past. Instead, I wanted her to hear from me that she was illegitimately conceived, and that she was not the legitimate daughter of her stepfather. I therefore shared this information with her when she was about seven years old. I was also protective of her because I didn't want her to make the same mistakes I had made.

As a child, Myishia instinctively knew that her grandfather, my father, was also a same-gender loving man. Because "Uncle Joe" and her grandfather were in a live-in relationship from the time Myishia was born, up until my father's death in

1975, she readily gravitated to both of them." Serendipitously, as her mother, I had firsthand and practical experience with same- gender loving relationships. However, it wasn't until Myisha turned eighteen that I suspected Myishia had inherited this gene.

Regrettably and retrospectively, I discovered later in life, and by then her pain was so great that by the time she was fifteen she resorted to drinking. Her enigmatic behavior became evident in high school when I was called to her school to hear that she had attempted suicide. This was so shocking to me because I was ignorant of her ongoing pain. As her mother, we followed through with therapy to no avail. Even then, she never revealed the internal struggle she had living a lie as a same-gender loving woman when she was not. As time went on, while she was in college, she ultimately revealed her sexual orientation to me. However, not knowing that she had escalated from drinking to drugging, her behavior was everything I detested, especially in a female. She brought home "strange" friends to whom I could not relate, since they appeared to be apathetic about their careers or future as responsible adults. In actuality, I was livid about her choice of friends more than her sexual orientation. To clear up my confusion and anger, I immediately engaged a therapist to help me. My first thought as a mother was, "What did I do to cause this?" After engaging in a few sessions with a certified clinical psychologist, I was relieved of any personal guilt.

In retrospect, I know Myishia tried hard to be heterosexual. In order to camouflage her sexuality and please me, she would date young men who were interested in her, attend heterosexual parties, and wear the girly or sexy dresses I bought and imposed upon her. I never knew how hypocritical she felt or how miserable she really was. My emotional and persistent response to Myishia's behavior ultimately caused her to search for a less stressful life and to escape from the rigidity that I, her mother, had imposed. Consequently, for more than three decades, we had an erratic relationship!

For years, research has been conducted on the origins of homosexuality. To date, it has been concluded that scientists have yet to produce firm evidence on its origin. However, there is consistency that sexual orientation is fundamental to a person rather than the lifestyle choice some opponents of equality suggest. To this day, I continue to research and digest its cause, which has helped me to move out of my own way and love my daughter unconditionally.

The Circle of Love: A Daughter's View

Myishia later revealed to me that while in the foster home, she would eagerly await by the window for me to appear. She would be so excited to see me that I truly felt valued by her innocent and unadulterated love. She would run to me, hug me, and place her small hand in mine as though somehow I would disappear if she let it go. Years later, when I questioned Myishia about this experience, she stated, "I really wanted to come home and stay with you at Maya's house; I didn't like my home in foster care and so looked forward to your arrival."

It is interesting to recall, at the immature age of fifteen, that I only looked forward to retrieving my daughter on the weekend. I didn't give much thought to how she may have been treated while under the foster family's care. In retrospect, my recollection is that I was never invited into the house in which she stayed as a foster child. Myishia was simply passed over to me without much of an exchange in words. If I knew then what I know now, I probably would have insisted on seeing her environment.

Later in life, Myishia expressed to me how she felt as a three-year-old while in foster care. She said, "I realized how much I adored you, depended on you, and idolized you. You were my goddess, my world, the mother that loved me and rescued me from my painful, dark, environment in foster care."

During the past thirty years, while we were estranged, we both transitioned into healthier, considerate, and more understanding women. We have finally accepted each other for who we are and not who we want each other to be. Today, the love between Myishia and me has come full circle. Over the latter part of our lives, I can honestly say we have developed a truly authentic mother-daughter bond. Because of this bond, I learned more about my daughter and her plight as a same-gender loving woman than a mother of a heterosexual child may know about her adult child. Because we are only fifteen years apart, we have become best friends.

During our numerous intimate conversations, Myishia shared that she knew she was attracted to a same-gender loving person when she was about six years old, but she did not know how to share this revelation with me. She felt that I would be disappointed in her, perhaps angry, and that I might reject her as my daughter. Consequently, she learned to internalize her feelings and thoughts about how she perceived the world around her. She revealed that she was in a tremendous amount of pain and on a slow suicide mission. Because she could not relate to how people in her era, the late 1960s and 1970s, felt about same-gender loving relationships, her secret life caused her to constantly experience the pain of rejection.

She felt that she simply was not good enough for her family to accept her. She legitimized these feelings by comparing herself to other same-gender loving people in the family. Not only was my father gay, there were also same-gender loving family members on her stepfather's side. Her thoughts and feelings led her to wonder why she, too, couldn't be accepted.

As a child, Myishia cherished family until she started to experience what she perceived as the family's rejection. As a teenager and young adult, she was teased, talked about, and ostracized. This was when she began to rebel and withdraw from the family by retreating into herself. This is when she began her painful journey of active addiction. Eventually, she left home and addiction took over her life.

Later on in her healthy life, she told me this:

"I believe the rejection I experienced as a teenager and young adult left a deeply rooted emotional scar; my sexuality issues simply exacerbated the scar. Nonetheless, had I not been perceived as different or a same-gender loving woman, what would be different? What I do know is that I would still have the wonderful memories of my childhood which would still be etched in my heart as great times! I was very fortunate as a child, and I know that now! I also believe, had I not been a same-gender loving woman, the impact of the family tensions would not have been as intense. I say this because I would not have been as scarred as I am today with memories of rejection."

What's important about *The Circle of Love: The Union Between a Mother and Her Same- Gender Loving Daughter* is highlighting the significance of a lack of love and how it affects our entire lives. In order to passionately love another human being, especially your same-gender loving child, regardless of our differences, we must first move out of our own way. Life is an attitude! Therefore, it is solely up to us to consistently measure our levels of happiness, source of contentment, satisfaction, or dissatisfaction in the life we live. Once we complete this self- evaluation, no matter where our results fall, we must then reach out to others whom we may feel are barriers to our joy and peace. We must finally take action to move out of our own ways to attain the love of those most important to us, regardless of our differences.

Carole F. Hysmith, EdD, is Chief Executive Officer of The Hysmith Group, Inc., a multi-service leadership, management, and career development company founded in 1991. The company is known for its expertise in organizational change by developing leadership and management teams as well as empowering staff.

Dr. Hysmith has more than thirty-five years of experience in education and development. During this time, she has provided extensive consultant services to senior executives regarding leadership and issues in organizational change. She has also worked for the New York City Health and Hospitals Corporation for nearly fourteen years, where she held various directorial positions in the training, career development, and organizational departments, working her way up to an appointment as deputy executive director of the Division of Human Relations for the Northern Manhattan Network of New York City Health and Hospitals Corporation.

Her professional background also includes experience as an instructor at Baruch College, a consultant at Marymount College, and ten years as an adjunct professor at the College of New Rochelle. She also served as an adjunct professor at Shorter College, School of Professional Programs, located in Atlanta, Georgia.

Dr. Hysmith earned a Masters of Arts in Organization Psychology from Columbia University and her EdD in organization development from the University of Massachusetts at Amherst. She is also certified in administering the Myers Briggs Type Indicator® as well as the 360-Degree Feedback Instrument.

MITOCHONDRIAL SEMANTICS

Michelle Dowell-Vest

My mother lives with me. For the last fifteen years, in every home I have had, with every partner I have loved, she has lived with me. In the forty-one years I have been alive, this is the longest span of time we have been together.

It's complicated.

In 1967, when my mother was eighteen, she gave birth to my oldest sister. But in 1973, the state removed my mother's parental rights, and my sister was placed for adoption. I don't know much about what happened, but if she mothered her like she mothered us, I'm sure it was because of severe neglect and abuse. I have only met Tabitha once in my life.

The Strength of My Soul

I was born a year later. After me, my mother had three more children—five total—while on welfare. In order to keep her welfare benefits, the state of California ordered my mother to undergo sterilization. Eugenics is a complicated historical practice of regulating who is worthy to reproduce and who is not. Its victims were always poor and most often women of color. In 1982, many would have believed this practice to be outlawed, but many states, including California, practiced limitations on family size with women who received state welfare benefits. In 1982, my mother was a victim of eugenics.

My mother often spoke of being the black sheep of her family. She felt constant rejection from her mother, and the pain from that translated to a life of addiction, self-loathing, and toxic mothering to both my siblings and me. I can distinctly remember the five times I lived with my mother when I was a child. The rest of my childhood was spent in and out of foster homes, where I endured physical, emotional, and sexual abuse.

When I was thirteen, living in a foster home, I attended a friend's slumber party. We decided to go skating, and there I met a twenty-year-old man, whom I started to date. We snuck around for a few weeks, but my foster parents didn't approve of him being so much older. So I convinced the child welfare system to let me go home to live with my mother so he and I could be together. I thought I loved him, and I knew my mother would let me be with him. Even though he knew I would not be safe in my mother's home, he also knew that he would have unfiltered access to me, so he encouraged me to go live with her. It was the quintessential story of a young girl thinking an older man could rescue her from the chaos of her home. Let's remember, I was thirteen.

Within a year I had given birth to my first child and we were married. Within a couple of months of my leaving my mother's home, my three younger siblings were removed from her custody after they were found hungry, abandoned, and sexually abused during one of her extensive drug binges. They were immediately placed for adoption and the state of California ruled her an unfit mother.

I was fourteen when I gave birth to my first child, fifteen when I had my second, and nineteen when I had my third. I married my children's father to escape life with my mom, and the next five years were a mix of high school, diapers, bottles, control, manipulation, emotional abuse, and a struggle to learn how to balance, survive, and thrive in it all.

Despite taking excellent care of my children, my home, finishing high school, and holding a full-time job, my ex-husband constantly reminded me of my upbringing. He convinced me that I was a horrible mother, that I was unfit, and that he would take my children if I ever left him. It was his way of beating down my confidence, my spirit, and my will.

He reminded me that I had no support system, and that because my mother was crazy and unfit (his words, not mine), I must be the same. After five years of being force-fed this message, I believed him. It would take me a long time to admit that my children's father was a sexual predator who took advantage of me. At thirteen, I was vulnerable. It wasn't until I saw him repeat the same pattern in other relationships with other young women that I saw him and our relationship for what they were.

When I was nineteen, I left my husband, and, more significantly, I left my children. I began to believe that I was the person he said I was. I had no home to take them to. I had no support system to help me. I thought I could leave, get on my feet, and then return for them. But it didn't work out that way. Like my mother, I was the daughter of an addict. Like her, I experienced pain, neglect, and abuse as a child. Like her, I was forced to figure life out on my own. Like my mother, I would make bad choices in relationships. Like her, I would make choices that left my children vulnerable. Like my mother, I would abandon my children. Like my mother, I would carry significant guilt about how I mothered my children.

Over the next ten years under his control, my unwillingness to fight back, my need to reclaim my teenage years, and my insatiable need to flee from guilt and shame led to the abandonment of my children. One day in early April of 1994, my children woke up with a mother and went to bed without one. I imagined what my children's faces looked like the day their dad told them I left. Today, this image still hurts my soul when I think of it. I never wanted to hurt them. I will always remember this feeling. Of course, it wasn't until the last couple of years that I could actually own the fact that I did abandon them.

As a child, every time I was taken away from my mother, my world shattered. I spent years in denial that I had caused this kind of pain in my children. I convinced myself that they were better off without me and better off with their father. I believed it would be unloving and selfish to try and get them back. After all, why would I disrupt their stability? I did a good job of convincing myself that leaving was best for them.

In the ten years I was apart from my children, I saw how my mommy issues manifested through my relationship with my own children. I didn't always make the best decisions regarding my children. I wasn't brave enough to face their father or his family and fight for them. I was a coward and decided that my comfort and my freedom were more important. Even though custody and visitation were more than frustrating and were many times denied, I have to own that I gave up and stopped fighting. I let him win. I let him create the narrative about who I was and why I left. I let my children down. I failed them. In this, I am just like my mother. I have had to own that.

Just as it can take generations for dysfunction to become mitochondrial, it also takes generations for it to be reversed. I repeated some of my mother's patterns, and my mother's mother and her mother's mother. I have done it in ways that are just now starting to manifest in my children's lives. I own that truth. And I also own the truth that sometimes I'm clueless about how to fix it.

It has been ten years since my two oldest children came back into my life, and we are constantly working to heal our open wounds. My children are now twenty-two, twenty-six, and twenty-seven. They are not babies anymore, and the dynamics have changed. In conversations with my daughter, I learn about the impact of lost mother-daughter moments and the ways I left her vulnerable. We are on good terms, and we work through stuff as it comes up. My oldest son is plagued with demons of inadequacy and abandonment while literally fighting for his sanity. Even today, he battles mental illness. As for my youngest son, we are working on getting to know each other. When I left his father, he was only ten months old. His stepmother raised him, and they have a close relationship.

As I write this, my daughter is working on her childhood baggage and forging a new relationship with her generational curse of dysfunction. She is committed to uprooting it. My relationship with my oldest son is frustrated and in a state of boundary setting, tough love, guilt management, crying, and navigation of the legal and mental health system. My youngest son and I desire to have a deeper relationship, but I think neither of us knows how to move forward. We are sweet and casual with each other. But I have this constant feeling that I am an inconvenience in his life. But, at least I am in it. I am showing up the best way I know how. I am showing up in my imperfections, my history of selfishness, and my desire to make it better.

Familial dysfunction is generational, and it anchors itself in our DNA. This is why it can be so hard to change our patterns. It takes persistence, patience, personal conviction, and a deep desire to love. But even with all of that, it can linger. My relationship with my mother still lingers. It lingers in the crevices of my memories and my constant battle with mom guilt and daughter pain. It lingers, and I can't say that it will ever go away. It also lingers in recipes and stories of raising hamsters and holidays at Nana's house. It wasn't all bad. But it all still lingers. She was my mom. She was meant to linger.

I share this story for the women out there who still have lingering stuff.

I am resisting the desire to wrap this up in a neat,

pretty bow, because sometimes our mess needs to be left untied and unmanaged. Sometimes our most powerful stories come from the middle of it all. And sometimes, the calm is ushered by sharing our frailty and imperfection. We live in a society that esteems perfection but exists in a reality that does not allow it.

I write this for the women in the middle of their storm – the women who need to know that in all their imperfections and sorting of their mess, there is beauty. It's okay to sit in our mess. We need to sit with it so we can feel it, digest it, and understand it, and when we have a full understanding of it, we can shed the pain and keep the memory and lesson.

My mother lives with me. Her being here is representative of me being in the middle of my mess with my own children. She is the constant reminder that I have to show up better. She is also my constant reminder that I am okay, that I am doing it better than she did. She wants me to know that. She speaks to me when I'm being extra hard on myself. I can hear her in my heart saying, "Michelle, I never got to this place. I'm proud of you. It will be okay. Michelle, I'm sorry." Maybe one day, I can let her rest, but until then, she has a job to do. She is here to remind me that it's okay.

I promised my mom that in her death she would always have a home with me. So, when she died in October 2000, I brought her ashes home with me and she has lived with me ever since. She sits in a gorgeous urn atop a shelf and has held a place in every home I have lived since 2000. I believe she watches over me and even visits my daughter on occasion. I think in her afterlife, she tries to care for me in ways she couldn't when she was alive.

I brought my mother home with me out of the guilt and co-dependency I learned as a child. I kept her with me because, over the years, her presence forced me to work out my anger toward her. This was the first time in my life that she was present with me. It's almost as if we were in therapy together. Truth be told, I also keep her with me to help me feel better about myself. I keep her here to remind me that I am doing better than she was able to. She motivates me.

I told you, it's complicated.

Michelle A. Dowell-Vest is a writer, community reporter, and random ranter. She is the creator of *A Gurlz Guide* and Podcaster with The Back2Us Radio Network. Both of these organizations are rooted in the belief that healing happens in community rather than in solitude, and that having space for our voice is liberating to both self and community.

In January 2016, she is launching *CitiNOOKS.com*. CitiNOOKS marries what she loves, what she wants to do more of, and what she is passionate about: Writing, travel, and inspiring others. CitiNOOKS.com is an online travel agency and magazine focused on inspiring others to travel more and often. Afterall, the world is expecting us.

More important than what she does is who she is. Michelle is the wife to Terésa Dowell-Vest, mother to three adults, and nona to six perfect grand babies. She strives to live a life of transparency, compassion, and intersectionality.

Michelle has always been an overcomer. Her life started with the adversity of, being born to an absent father and a drug addicted mother and having to face the unique challenges that came with being tossed from one foster home to another. Triumphant over physical, sexual, and emotional abuse, she learned she has the power to heal and transform her life. When she grew tired of repeating the same destructive patterns of toxic relationships, she committed to the difficult road of emotional healing and declared that she was not a victim.

In her healing, Michelle learned that life is a constant flow of change, and that in order to overcome adversity in a healthy way, one has to understand the ebb and flow of loss, grief, love, and joy. Life's a balancing act that can be amazing if we make the choice to invest in our healing, to harness the power of our intuition, and to understand the value in the collective energy of the community around us.

You can find Michelle on Twitter @AGurlzGuide"

BECOMING... ME

Valerie Hall

At forty-six years old, I'm not even sure if I will ever really "arrive," but I have come to realize that I am exactly where and who I am meant to be. I am supposed to be constantly growing and changing, evaluating, and flowing toward whomever the Universe/God has intended me to be. Sometimes I am excited to know what it will all look like in the end. Will I have gray hair and enjoy the company of grandchildren? Will I get to look at my only child on his fifty-fifth birthday, feeling a mother's pride? Will I have a loving partner by my side, holding my hand as we navigate into our twilight years together?

Who am I? Why do I think the way that I think? Why do I act and react the way that I do to situations or experiences? And why did I spend so many years feeling as if I'd been doing it all wrong somehow?

Perhaps part of my issue is that I was nearly forty years old before I ever considered being kind to myself, before I ever thought to cut myself the same slack or offer myself the same level of understanding that I do to anyone that I care about. I was nearly forty years old before I ever really acknowledged to myself that I had lived most of my years wearing a façade, even when I was alone – that even with no one else around to care, it has always been important for me to display that I was "okay," to somehow prove that I was too strong for anyone to hurt me, or simply that I didn't "need" anyone for anything. Because of this, I have been called cold, distant, aloof, and even mean, when nothing could be further from the truth. I care. I care too much.

As a highly empathetic person, I have struggled with experiencing not only my own deep feelings or emotions, but also, far too often, I feel the pain, anguish, and unhappiness of others. When someone cries, I am too quick to join him or her in that pain. When someone is angry or anxious, I often become solemn or anxious myself. Far too often I find myself going deeply inward, and it was not that long ago that I identified what I was doing, exercising a perfected habit of self-protection. Detaching from others or merely compartmentalizing my touchy-feely soft parts into tidy little silos that I could manage without feeling completely overwhelmed or like I was drowning in the dark and murky depth of so much raw emotion.

It took me a lot of time and tons of therapy to realize why I am a control freak, why I often feel like I am the only one I can count on for important decisions or to do the right thing, why succeeding or excelling in my career is so important to me, or why I chose it to be the primary measure of my happiness. It took me even longer to understand why I have a hard time trusting any person or circumstance. And it took me way too long to really understand that this lack of trust isolated me and kept me from building true and sustainable relationships with family, friends, and lovers. Sure, these connections existed, but they were often thin as parchment while I constantly longed for the ironclad bonds that I saw others experience. Yet it was always me that prevented these bonds from forming.

It was only when I started to see my last counselor, Linda, that I really began to examine myself as an adult woman. I stopped identifying as my mother's child, my son's mother, my company's employee, my significant other's lover, etc. Instead, I started to focus on *me*. During one of my sessions with Linda, she asked me one truly life-altering question. This question ended up being the catalyst of so much change for me, of so much change *within* me. The question she asked was pretty simple: "Valerie, when was the last time that you felt safe?" And, once asked, she gave me until our next weekly session to provide my answer to her because she really wanted me to be honest with myself in my reply. I drove home and spent that entire week thinking deeply about when I last felt truly safe and when I answered it inside my own head. It hurt a little. It hurt to realize that the last time I felt truly safe was probably when I was ten years old.

I was blessed with a pretty good memory. Whether recalling my first tricycle, my first day of school, or a lecture in freshman English class, I have always been able to close my eyes and "see" that memory like a home movie replaying in my mind. When I sum up my memories of childhood, I can say with a smile on my face that until I was about ten, my life was quite ordinary, but in my memories and in my heart it was perfect back then! My family consisted of a military dad, a stay-at-home mom, two kids, and a dog. We were an active family that enjoyed doing things together, traveled on summer vacations, and laughed. A lot. I was taught to play tennis and to swim. I was encouraged to do things like play softball, learn ballet, compete in gymnastics, and just have fun! My parents were there to watch and cheer me on, and when I recall those memories, I am happy. I understood my life then. I was loved and cherished, and above all things, I felt safe. Truth be told, until about that age, I thought my daddy hung every star in the sky for my mom, my younger brother, and me. He was our provider, our protector, and my hero. I watched him love my mother and knew that when I grew up, that was the sort of love I wanted for myself.

But when I was ten, my dad started to drink heavily. The occasional beer after work or the social drinking I'd seen him do during gatherings with family and friends turned into empty whiskey bottles and beer cases. Our home, once filled with laughter, became a set of four walls, with floors made of fragile eggshells. My brother and I were now children to be seen and not heard, since to do otherwise risked setting off my dad. It was about that age that I remember first hearing him yell at my mother in a drunken stupor, calling her names that no reasonable man would ever use within ear's reach of his two children, let alone aimed at his devoted wife.

By the time I was eleven, those mean words spoken when drunk turned into full-blown rages that involved him beating my mother to the ground and inflicting bloody noses, black eyes, and bruises that still make me flinch to recall. Most of this happened as I watched, and because they kept happening, I learned to beg, plead, and cry for him to leave my mother alone. Because she never fought back, not even verbally, I was actively fighting my father on her behalf before I turned twelve. I had figured out how to hit him with something heavy enough to snap him out of his stupor, to distract him just long enough for him to look at me while I fought to focus my face and hear the words that I was yelling at him. I had learned to say the right words to make him feel just enough shame to stop what he was doing, at least long enough for me to gather up my mother and then my younger brother and put them both in my bed. I had figured out how to use a shoestring from my sneakers to lace a lock of sorts around my bedroom doorknob, ensuring he could not come in and hurt us, at least not that night. I had figured out how to go to school the next day without sleeping much at all the night before. I had learned to keep secrets.

During those years, there were so many occasions for which I needed my father. One night, I accidentally locked myself outside on our patio during a desert thunderstorm, completely terrorized by the lightning and the booming thunder but determined to console my dog Misty, whom I'd heard crying and whimpering in her doghouse outside. Soaking wet with chattering teeth, I yelled over and over for my daddy to open the door, to come and rescue me! But I knew he was drunk before he'd gone to bed. When the storm finally quieted down, my mother, not him, found me. I will never forget what it felt like to be hoarse from screaming "Daddy!" over and over, and how it felt to realize he just wasn't coming. There was also the time that I'd flipped myself over the handlebars of my brand new ten-speed bicycle and limped into the house, only to find him passed out on the sofa. Mom wasn't home that day, so I cleaned and bandaged myself in the hall bathroom, constantly looking at him laying nearby on the couch, trying to will him awake with my mind, silently begging him to do something, to simply care for me again.

My pre-teen years were filled with nights in which

I slept with the lights on, hid in the back of my closet afraid, or stayed awake all night believing it was my job to watch over my mother and my baby brother. So many nights I cried myself to sleep after having horrible nightmares filled with painful memories, those endless nights when nobody came and no one comforted me. That feeling takes a toll on one's spirit and her them to comfort herself. This I know all too well.

What I also know is that by the time I was a teenager, I had learned to lie. I had learned to deny. I had learned to pretend, to simply declare to the world that everything was okay. Doing so seemed the only way to make my young heart understand what had become of my life, of my family. By that time, all of the fun stuff we had once done together was just memory. We all simply knew that if Daddy started drinking, a fight was guaranteed. My mom, brother, and I fell into a pattern of exemplary behavior, doing all that we could to improve his mood to avoid a fight or at least minimize how bad the fighting would be. Truth be told, I can't even tell you when the raging and fighting stopped. I do know that we'd gone to family counseling. I know that my father had made a conscious decision to no longer drink "hard liquor." I also know that by the time I was fourteen, my parents had tried their hand at legal separation. But I also remember that despite everything, I still lived for those moments when I could make my dad proud of me. I actively sought out his approval, but it had been many years since that man had expressed any kind or even cordial words to me. Even now, at forty-six, I still miss him. Unfortunately, seeking approval or acceptance has been something I've struggled with for most of my life.

Yes, I enjoyed much of my childhood. I do remember feeling loved, cared for, and safe. Because I enjoyed so many of my early years feeling so good about my life, the hurt I felt when that life became filled with rage and fear burned like a red hot poker into my most tender places, and that pain stayed with me far longer than I'd like to admit. The pain and related negligence taught me that I was the only one I could depend on. It taught me that my life didn't include protectors or heroes, and that those things belonged only to the good little girls from good little families, girls I saw only on television or in the movies. If I had to describe what my teenage years felt like, I would use one word: empty. I simply went through the motions of living with my family. I did what was expected of me, bided my time, and left the house the moment I was done with school. I have been on my own ever since, never again living with my mom. I was fifteen the last time I shared a home with my one and only brother. And truthfully, I have only seen him perhaps twenty times since then, with many years going by without us even speaking to each other. This was all because when our parents split up, I went with my mom and he went with my dad. Unfortunately, time has not healed that rift. Perhaps we have all simply learned to be without one another; to do without; to deny that it causes pain or hurt; to live as if it doesn't matter; to pretend, just like we did as children.

During my counseling sessions with Linda, I finally faced some pretty cold facts. I had taken childhood feelings of abandonment, shame, secrecy, and loneliness well into my adult years and had allowed them to become stronger than the love I felt for others. I had allowed them to devour my desire for human connection and allowed them to convince me that I could live my life without ever needing anyone. I truly believed that being alone was easier than depending on anyone else, or that being alone or isolating my heart would somehow ensure a life without disappointment or pain. Foolish, isn't it? It's foolish because I still hurt, a lot. Foolish because I have come to know that the human condition guarantees our need to love and to be loved. God built us this way, and it is truly undeniable.

When I returned to Linda's office and told her that I was about ten years old the last time I truly felt safe and shared with her the history that I share with you within these pages, it was she that helped me to construct a sort of road map of what it would look like to feel safe again in my life. This roadmap included practical things that I could do for myself to feel secure. It included ways for me to separate my needs and wants as a mother or a daughter and pinpoint what Valerie, the woman, would need to be happy and feel safe in life. It was the first time that I allowed myself to admit that I had a deep need to love and be loved by someone within the construct of an authentic and sustaining romantic relationship. It was then that I promised myself I would no longer settle for relationships that were "just enough." I would no longer allow myself to choose partners who were safe only because I would let myself open up to them or risk much at all to be with them. I wanted to be vulnerable, and I wanted to be real. I wanted to allow myself to be truly seen and heard and let another heart love me through all of that. I wanted others to rely on me, and I wanted to rely on others.

It's been nearly five years since I made that conscious decision. I've explored people and circumstances, I've explored myself, and I've explored my reactions to those people and those circumstances. I get it wrong a lot. But, as I continue to grow, I am coming to truly understand that simply wanting something does not prepare you to deal with it once it's yours. I've experienced the whole "be careful what you ask for" phenomenon many times over and found myself lacking, confused, and even frustrated, and I am absolutely sure that I've caused these same feelings in others.

Yet I am exactly where I am supposed to be. I am the sum of many parts, and I am still learning, still healing, and still growing. I will never forget the girl I once was, but I can treat the woman that I am becoming with grace and understanding as I continue to get it right sometimes and make a mess of it sometimes, too. I've lived a long time with many regrets, but the moment I chose to no longer feel shame about my past, it began to actually *help* me move forward. The moment I chose to give myself the gifts of forgiveness and hope and the moment I allowed myself to take the risk of loving deeply and authentically were the moments I stopped merely existing and truly started to live.

Yes, it has taken time and many false starts and abrupt stops, but eventually, I attracted the love that I'd been searching for. This love is strong and overwhelming yet so incredibly tender that it makes my heart swell. I share my life now with someone who sees and hears me, and while we still have miles to go on our journey together, I can tell you that loving without holding back and leaving some things strictly to faith and hope have been life altering, strengthening, and affirming. I chose the right thing for myself, and this love makes me feel as if I am finally reaping my rewards. As deeply as she loves and cares for me, she also challenges me and makes me constantly reevaluate how to make what I want and need to work within a relationship of *two* different perspectives and life experiences. All of this is done so we are both seen and heard. Lastly, she sees some of the remaining fractures of my family life, and she actively does and says things that help us all work toward more healing. Everything that I would do for others, she does for me. Who would have ever thought I deserved such love, that I deserved to reap what I have sown? It truly is a blessing!

Do you find yourself feeling stuck, or like something is holding you back from living the life you dream for yourself? If so, perhaps it is time for you to dig deeply, find your old wounds, look them square in their frightening faces, and demand that they let you go! This was the first step that helped me most. Acknowledging where I came from has brought me such clarity and has helped me build the roadmap to where I want to be, to the *person* I want to be. It will be a life- long process of building, working hard, and growing. But when you are working for your own dreams and happiness, you will always know it is time well spent. We deserve our best, from others surely, but from ourselves as well.

Yes, we *all* deserve to become our best and finest selves.

Valerie Hall is a forty-something professional in the IT industry. Often called on for her expertise in corporate communications, as well as for IT Service Manage Operations and Service Delivery, she is a highly skilled technical writer who tends to write more personal pieces that simply flow from her heart.

She is the oldest child of four and the only daughter in a blended family. She has one adult son who is her pride and joy and is currently engaged to be married sometime in 2015 or 2016. Valerie has been writing all of her life, but this will be the first venture she's taken toward publishing, and she is incredibly excited for this part of her writing journey!

I Made It Despite The Odds

IF I CAN, YOU CAN: DETERMINATION!

Anjelis Oliveira

Standing over my *tia*, the only mother figure I knew, while she was lying on a hospital bed fighting for her life, was a life-changing moment in my young life. After spending a few moments with her in the hospital room, I was kicked out of the hospital. According to my family, l was the culprit of her condition because she had discovered I was sexually active! Yes, I had caused her misfortune. I was made to believe that she was so hurt by my behavior that she had a stroke, and my family was unrelenting. They were adamant: I had caused her illness. Because of my behavior, my *tia* was lying there helpless on that bed!

My family made sure that I knew and felt totally responsible for the pain, discomfort, and any other medical consequence that might occur because of her stroke. It was my fault. It may have been heartbreaking, but I would have to live with it.

At that moment, I realized I no longer belonged to this family. I recall that shortly after she recovered from her stoke, I became distant and detached from them all. I was cautious, afraid to upset her. After all, I had been convinced that soon I would cause her to die. I could not live with myself if anything happened to her, so I stayed away; I retreated and tried to deal with the guilt, the isolation, and the sadness.

Two days before my sixteenth birthday, I was left to fend for myself when my *tia* was flown to the Dominican Republic to recover from the stroke that she had suffered three months prior. A few days after she left to the Dominican Republic, my uncle and his family picked me up, and everything I knew was ripped from under me. School changed, sports were forbidden, and I was forced to share a house with a group of people, supposedly my family, that deep down enjoyed my struggles and took pleasure when I fell. Unfortunately, my new accommodations only lasted a few months because I never felt as if I belonged in my uncle's house or in the family. On July 1st, 1998, I moved out; I left my uncle's home and moved to a twin bed in a corner of a room at the house of a family friend. It wasn't paradise, but I had peace.

Soon after, my warm, welcome feeling would not last there either. It dissolved after only a few weeks. I somehow sensed that living at that house would not be my home for much longer! Living at the family friend's house was better than living with my uncle, but it definitely was not home. It was a time of survival, filled with internal struggles as I tried to find a way to overcome so much adversity. I wanted to prove to so many people that my life would mean something, even if I didn't know what that something was.

My life had not been easy. Fourteen years prior my mother had died in a tragic car accident. And even though my father was alive, he chose his fortune over me and assumed no responsibility for my care or upbringing. I felt as if I had no one to love me, and in many ways, I felt like an orphan. I was constantly moved from household to household, from relative to relative, without any concern about my feelings, needs, or well-being. Nobody took interest in what the constant moves and changes were doing to my psyche. And so, I never felt loved. I felt shunned, let down, blamed, threatened, insulted, and bullied.

And when it seemed as if it couldn't get any worse, the unthinkable happened. One night, my cousin fondled me. While he did it, he whispered in my ear that I was a slut anyway, so it didn't matter. When I threatened to scream and wake anybody up, he stopped. Of course, I was traumatized. I felt dirty, ashamed, and guilty.

Later, I wrote a letter in the dark addressed to no one, asking for help and telling everyone I knew that being touched inappropriately was *not* my fault. I tossed the letter since I knew no one would believe me anyway. I was never able to tell anyone what my cousin did, because I was afraid no one would believe me. I still recall the impotence I felt that night!

Every experience made me feel unworthy, and my family's lack of concern only deepened those feelings. Why should I exist? What was the point of so much pain? Why would God waste life on an insignificant being like me? If my own father didn't want me, who in his right mind would?

In the midst of my internal struggles to find the meaning of my existence, and in the midst of surviving alone at sixteen, I met Edgar. Edgar was a charming boy who had many problems of his own, but he accepted me and wanted me.

Initially, I didn't understand why Edgar liked me, and I probably overlooked many of what I now know are red flags. But he wanted me, and that was all that seemed to matter. For the first time in my life, I felt wanted!

Edgar and I were both running away from our demons; we both had troubled pasts. Yet in less than three months, we moved in together and started new lives. Two months later, I was overjoyed with the news that I was pregnant. Unfortunately, I suffered a heartbreaking miscarriage, caused by the beatings I received from Edgar. Pushing, kicking, choking, and punching, Edgar, the charming boy who wanted me, constantly abused me! I endured the hits, punches, and verbal attacks. After the trauma of the miscarriage, I hoped the abuse would stop, but it continued. Maybe deep down inside I felt I deserved the beatings. I thought they were the price I had to pay to be wanted.

While I recovered from the miscarriage, I missed a few weeks of advanced placement courses in school. I fell behind in my assignments, and, as a result, was forced to transfer to adult education classes at night. The plan was to go back to school for my senior year, but eventually I dropped out because I got pregnant again and was too ashamed to return. In June of 2000, the first true love of my life came into the world. After a traumatic and abusive pregnancy, I felt blessed that my baby arrived healthy and in one piece! It was a feeling I had never felt before. I had another human being that I would give my life for ten times over. I had someone who depended on me to survive!

One month after giving birth to my son, I recall my grandmother rescuing me. I was extremely malnourished because I was breastfeeding and not eating well. Eating saltine crackers throughout the day was my main source of nourishment because I had no food and no assistance.

I was eighteen and recovering from a C-section, and I had no social support and a nonexistent husband. The day my newborn son and I went to visit my grandmother, she would not let us leave; she was afraid I wouldn't make it if I continued living that way. I should also mention that my "family" lived a door down from me during that time but refused to offer any assistance. They didn't care.

After I had Jose, I wanted to do everything I could to give him a better life than the one I had had. I knew I had to be strong and make my family work despite the repeated abuse and infidelities. A few months after my son was born, my husband almost stabbed me with a knife. But I had to stay, right? I had a son! Despite that event and so many incidents, I thought to myself, "I was lucky he wanted me. Surely nobody else did!" Two years later, Alexander was born and I finally felt like my family was complete. I was tired of the abuse, but I felt I had survived. I knew that with the arrival of my new son, I could die and my kids would at least have each other! I would never let what had happened to me happen to them.

It was after I had given birth to Jose that I dedicated myself to improving my life. I got my GED, and then started to attend classes at Miami Dade College. While there, God sent me an angel, Victor. Victor was a tall, dark, and handsome sales representative who believed in me like no one ever had. Every day he would remind me how smart I was, asking me when I was going to start school. I registered ten days before the semester started just to shut him up!

During that time, I started to learn about domestic violence. I can still vividly recall the first time I realized that abuse was not okay. I was sitting in a Human Growth and Development class while the instructor lectured about battered women. I thought, "Oh my God, that is me!" Thankfully, my husband supported my school venture. He frequently encouraged me after one of his painful beating to finish school. He would say, "Go to school so you don't have to put up with this from another man!" How ironic.

It took a few more semesters, getting into nursing school, and a few dozen more beatings and infidelities for me to get out of the abusive cycle with my husband. But thank the Lord and my guardian angels, in December of 2003, I did! Granted, I did not know how I was going to pay the rent or feed my children, but I knew I had to leave for my sake and the sake of my children. So, in January of 2004, I made one of the hardest decisions of my life. I knew I would have to either quit school or send my children, my life, to the Dominican Republic until school was over. I was at a crossroads, and I knew the decision would change the trajectory of my life. After all, I felt like I was fortunate to have a choice, even if it wasn't ideal. Even though it was painful, I made a decision not only for my children but also for me – my growth and my purpose in life! I refused to be the failure my family wanted me to be. So I sent my kids to the Dominican Republic for a year and three months while I worked nights at the Jackson Memorial Hospital emergency department and finished nursing school during the day. I am proud to say that I finished at the top of my class. Magna Cum Laude, baby! Too bad no one was there to see me.

I cried during my graduation, not tears of joy but tears of sadness. It was difficult to accept that no one I loved had witnessed my great achievement. Again no one chose me. So many people were willing to be an audience for my failure, but none were willing to witness or be a part of my success! Secretly, though, I was thrilled. I had proven so many people wrong; I made it. My family would soon realize their insults actually fueled my desire to overcome the statistics. Despite the odds, I was successful!

After graduation, my kids came back to the United States and my life started again. However, I guess you can never run away from your past, not even at work. One morning, I heard a familiar voice screaming. It turned out my ex-husband's mistress, now-girlfriend, had been brought to the ER for attempting suicide after a fight with him. The staff was in the process of restraining her when I told them I knew her and would personally take care of her.

I was so appreciative to this girl for opening my eyes to the extent of my ex-husband's infidelities a few years earlier. After we had separated, my husband started using cocaine again, and even then I was actually considering going back to him because of my kids! To fulfill a faulty illusion of "family.", and I was actually considering going back! Yeah, and I thought I knew better by now, right? I guess part of me still felt I deserved the punishment and that I would not find anyone better. Lord, I was blind! Even though his mistress tried to hurt me by sharing my ex-husband's infidelities, I am I grateful. Exposing my ex-husband infidelities and sexual escapades probably saved my life!

Because I felt sorry for her, I took good care of her. She was in a bad place like I had been in not too long ago! I cared for her like she was my own family, and she of course showed her appreciation with a piercing, drunken apology to me (and the entire department) for taking my husband's side. She yelled in the top of her lungs, "I am sorry I took your husband!" Of course, I didn't need this drunken apology since we had already made amends when she told me the truth about the affair. Still, I was grateful for it. Now, her comment was not the highlight of my career, but I held my head up high, even in that moment of shame. After all, I had beaten the odds. I was a survivor!

After five years as a nurse, on a whim I started my master's degree at the University of Phoenix. A very dear friend of mine, another angel sent into my life, encouraged me to start school, and, as I did with Victor, I registered just to shut her up! But I am glad I did. The process was grueling, to say the least. In addition to school, I was working two jobs as a single mother of three beautiful boys. Regardless, three years later, I finished school with two masters degrees, which transformed my way of thinking and opened many doors professionally. Completing my education was my legacy to my children.

With more thought this time, I am currently enrolled at Barry University Doctor in Philosophy in Nursing program and am well underway to a terminal degree. I promised myself during my undergraduate graduation that some day I would wear the beautiful gown and the "funny little hat" across the stage. It may seem like a silly motivation to most, but it helped me to visualize getting through this program. Motivation is very personal and has to burn inside you, driving you to achieve your goals—any goal, not just educational ones!

Today, I believe that no one can take knowledge from you, not through beatings or insults! It may seem like a long time before you finish your education, but hey, time passes anyway. You might as well do something productive with it! Education costs a lot of money—of course it does—but you are worth it! And again, anyone can lose a car or a house, for whatever reason, but the knowledge and experiences you acquire are yours for life! So invest in yourself and make this life count because it's the only one you have!

We all have a purpose in life because the Lord doesn't make mistakes. My life and your life have meaning. Don't let it go to waste! You deserve all the beautiful things life has to offer, and now I know that I do, too. It was a struggle, with many low points, but in the end I survived. I survived not because I am strong, but because I made a choice not to allow anyone to keep me down! And you, too, can make this choice. Love yourself and know that although you cannot control what other people around you do to you or say about you, it's entirely up to you how you let it affect you.

Anjelis Oliveira graduated from Florida International University in 2005 with a Bachelors in Science in Nursing. After earning a Masters in Science in Nursing and Healthcare Administration from the University of Phoenix in 2013, she started pursuing a PhD in Nursing at Barry University. Through education, Anjelis has expanded not only her professional skills, but also personal skills.

Anjelis has dedicated her life to promoting wellness and advocating for patients in acute care and outpatient settings. Currently, she is a Nurse Manager in an academic institution in Miami, Florida, a position she has held for the past six years. Anjelis is a single mother of three amazing young men. This chapter is an excerpt from her upcoming book, *If I Can, You Can: A Story of Resilience, Determination, and Hope.*

YOU ALMOST BROKE ME

Ava Cary

It was the summer of 2006. I was awakened by a touch on my arm. I heard a small yet powerful voice calling out, "doctor, doctor! My mom's moving, and she's opening her eyes." Unaware of where I was, I had not realized that I was in a coma at the University of Pittsburgh Medical Center (UPMC). It had been four days since I had taken over forty pills and then grabbed a gun to end my life. If not for the pills rendering me weak, I would have shot myself in the head. Thank God the aim of the bullet hit the ceiling and not my head. After the incident, I opened my eyes and saw the doctor and nurses rushing into my room to check my vital signs. As my daughter held me and cried, both she and a friend stood by my bedside grabbing my hand with a look of relief and fear in their eyes.

The doctor explained that due the nature of my arrival at UPMC, I would be escorted by police officers to the eighth floor of the psychiatric ward. Still dazed and confused by what was happening, I wasn't sure whether I should be glad to be alive. While I lay there listening to everyone, I thought, should I thank God that I was alive, or was He punishing me for still being here? Why would He let someone experience this much trauma? What kind of God was He? Yes, I was angry with Him for allowing these things to happen to me.

Once inside the psychiatric unit, I was taken into a pure white room. There were no windows, just my thoughts, a bed, and me. As I lay there alone, reflecting back on the four days I was in a coma, I recalled being in an extremely bright place. It was similar to the room I was in, but more gleaming. To this day, I still believe that I died.

My thoughts then trailed off to what had landed me in the hospital. My life had seemed hopeless. I had come to a breaking point. The God that I had served my whole life had failed me. I had endured an abusive marriage that failed miserably. Having to flee my home to provide safety for my children, I found myself living in a battered women's shelter. I began to cry out to God, asking Him how He could allow one failed relationship after another. Ultimately, my past was filled with trauma. Where was God?

I fixated on my youth. The events of my childhood had led me to this place. Growing up in a small town in Kentucky, my whole life revolved around church. We attended the Church of the Living God Pillar Ground of Truth, a sanctified holiness church that my grandmother took us to every Sunday. The church owned a big brown van that traveled around town every Sunday morning to pick up members. Grandma would load me, my five siblings, and about ten to fifteen of my cousins in the old van every Sunday morning because going to church was not optional. If the church was having service, we were there and the van was always there to pick us up. Regardless of the day of the week, two things were consistent: church and the big brown van. Attending church was important, so the pastor himself would drive patiently from house to house to pick up members. Going to church was our reality and so we got in the overcrowded van and sang to the glory of God all the way to church. We would have a head-bopping, feet- stomping, Holy Ghost good time in the church van even before we even got to church.

But I could also recall when things began to change. As the original pastor and his wife, whom everyone seemed fond of, grew older, my family helped out around their home for whatever they needed. To ensure they got their exercise, I took them on walks. It was around that time we got news that a significant revival known as a "big top tent" was coming to town. This seemed to be the talk of the town because we had never seen or heard of anything like that before in our community. There were so many people coming from different cities into our town to celebrate God. And honestly, I never knew there were so many people who were "saved."

As a child, the only thing I knew was the church, so when my mom said we were going that night, I made sure I was ready when it was time to leave. The music was invigorating and could be heard from miles away. Hearing the music energized my spirit! I had never heard church music played so passionately. I was ready to "have church." In that tent, I could feel the spirit of the Lord; His presence was so powerful. The missionaries were dressed in their white gowns, flashing their aprons and praying the power of Jesus to come down over a sin-filled town. That very night, I walked up to the altar for the pastors to lay hands on me, which was a way to cleanse us and invite God into our hearts. As the pastors prayed for me, I felt how important I was to God. By the time they were done with me, I was saved. From that moment forward, my life was changed.

About two days later I got sick, and my fever was so high that I could not get out of bed. Some missionaries and preachers from the big top tent came to pray away the sickness, and their prayers worked. Their prayers worked so well that the very next day I was able to go back to the revival to testify about how God healed my little body. The saints were shouting and praising God with me. I knew I must have been something special to God for him to heal me. After the big top tent had left town, news came that a new church was being built for our congregation. A new pastor, too, had been selected, who now became a father figure to my family.

Shortly after that news came, my mom seemed different; she was not her usual self. That particular afternoon, I knew someone important was visiting the house, because normally we would have meals like pork and beans for dinner. But this afternoon was different. We were told to get the house in order while my mom cooked fried chicken, pork chops, collard greens, candied yams, macaroni and cheese, mashed potatoes, homemade rolls, and pineapple upside down cake for dessert. It smelled delicious. Soon, I learned that the new pastor of our church was coming for dinner.

Things continued to change around the house; the pastor always seemed to be around. I never minded because he would teach us kids how to do things my mother could never teach us. He taught us how to refinish cabinets, lay concrete, and paint. He was amazing; he was the father I never had. His daughter, Kenya, would even come over sometimes to hang out with my sisters and me. Kenya played a fundamental role in my life. She was like a big sister whom I could tell almost anything. Sometimes I would spend the entire night with her at her home. I would meet her mother on a few occasions, and I thought she had such a kind spirit, although it seemed odd that she only rarely went to the services, being a pastor's wife. As a young girl, I did not know to ask questions.

There was another oddity. When the pastor would come over, which he did frequently, he would go into my mother's room with my mother and close the door. I never questioned what was going on, since I assumed they were praying. I also never mentioned this secret to Kenya, because my mother's philosophy was that whatever happened in our home should stay in our home. If my mother found out that one of us kids told the household business, we would get a beating and then be on punishment.

Then, when I was sixteen years old, my life changed. My mom had given the pastor permission to pick me up from school early. As we drove to the church, he explained that he wanted to talk to me about some things. He mentioned that he wanted to discuss my position as Sunday school teacher and the director of the youth choir. While I did not think it was necessary to be picked up early from school to have those discussions, I didn't care. He made me feel important. Being picked up from school by the church pastor made me feel good about my Christian walk. I remember thinking God must be so proud of me for serving in church.

When we arrived at the church, I noticed he never turned the lights on once inside the church. This seemed strange, but this was my pastor, so I never questioned him. Instead of sitting in the sanctuary he took me to his office and closed the door. Rather than discuss church business, he began talking about my relationship with a boy from another local church. He wanted to know if we had ever been intimate. I felt his questioning was odd, and I started to feel uncomfortable. I thought, "Where is this conversation going?" Nevertheless, I explained to him that we, the boy and me, had never been intimate. The pastor then began to comment on my appearance. He said that my body looked like a twenty-five-year-old woman. I cringed, and I started to feel incredibly awkward and afraid. I knew his comments were inappropriate, or at least I felt that they should be; he was my pastor, and I was only teenager.

He slid closer to me as he explained that he wanted to teach me some things so that I would be prepared in life. He got up to lock the office doors, and as he approached me, he pulled his penis out of his pants. He then threw me over the office desk, pulled my skirt up and began to rub his penis between my thighs. I started to hit him and tried to push him off of me. I screamed and yelled for him to get off of me. He attempted to penetrate me, and then all of a sudden I could feel this wet, sticky feeling around my vagina. I

The Strength of My Soul

screamed for him to get off me and to please stop! As he stood there pulling up his pants, he turned to me and said, "Let's pray and ask God to forgive us."

Feeling traumatized, startled, and confused, I explained to him there was no reason for me to ask for forgiveness since I had not done anything wrong. I managed to leave the room and ran to the restroom where I locked myself in. Shortly after, he followed me there. He then started to knock on the door and asked me to come out and pray for God's forgiveness. I was crying and so confused; my whole life had changed. Eventually, I heard him walk away from the restroom door.

When all was quiet, I crept through the back kitchen door of the church. As soon as I opened the door, everything seemed so white, so surreal. I was numb; I could not believe what had just happened. I walked as fast as I could, and I did not stop until I got to my middle school. Once there, I hid in an abandoned school bus for hours as I tried to comprehend what had just occurred. I felt disgusted, dirty, betrayed, and lost. How could this have happened to me? Why did this happen to me? I thought, "God where were you?" This was my pastor, a man sent to watch over

God's children and me. As I tried to gather my thoughts, I felt like I was not in my body. I just sat there. I could not move and felt as if my life was at a standstill. I guess I was in shock because I could not even process what just happened. My pastor had just raped me.

I hid in the bus for hours as I attempted to gather myself. I am not sure how long I stayed in the bus, but it was getting dark when I left. When I got home, my mother asked me what had happened and where I had been. She asked, "Did the pastor do something to you?" My behavior must have indicated that something was wrong or at least out of the ordinary. But I did not feel safe confiding in my mother, and I did not want to share with her. This was not the first time I had been violated by someone who was close to my mom. In fact, years earlier my uncle had touched me inappropriately and nothing happened to him. He was not punished. So why should I tell her what happened? Why should I feel comfortable sharing with a person who had failed to protect me before? She gave the pastor permission to check me out of school, so why should I trust her?

Initially, I remained silent until my older sister, who had always been my protector, talked to me.

The Strength of My Soul

She asked me to tell her what had happened that afternoon. I shared with my mother and sister that the pastor had raped me. My sister wrapped her arms around me and tried to console me. My mother didn't move. She didn't hug me. She didn't even reach for me. Of course, this made me feel as if I had done something wrong, as if I was somehow responsible for my pastor's immorality. After sharing with my mom that my pastor had just assaulted me and violated me, she told me I had to attend church the next day. I felt alone.

Twenty years later, I received a phone call from a detective who had been speaking with my mother about the rape that had taken place in the church many years ago. I will probably never know the real reason the detective contacted me, nor will I know the truth of why my mother finally contacted the police. But for me, her support was twenty years too late. I wanted to leave my past in the past. I wanted to leave the experience behind me, even though I could never fully forget what happened. The incident stayed with me and lived in me—I could not shake it. And even though I did my best to forget, I constantly relived that unfortunate day. I continued to suffer from nightmares, but I knew I had to keep silent. What other choice did I have? I had been warned that

I'd be cursed if I spoke negatively about the pastor, so I had to keep quiet. I didn't want to suffer anymore; I had endured enough physical and emotional pain already. In twenty years, no one had ever asked the specific details about the rape before, so why the questions now?

After twenty years of nightmares and sadness, the painful memories flooded my mind and spirit. I wanted to forget about the pastor, my hometown, and that day. Needing direction and spiritual counseling, I immediately called my new pastor and shared these secrets. I didn't know what to do, feel, or say, and I desperately needed guidance. My new pastor explained that for my protection it might be better for me to speak with a female minister. When I finally spoke with her, I shared my deepest, darkest moment in the hope of receiving some counseling or at least some consoling. I cried hysterically as I tried to recount all of the hurt and pain of the circumstance. In the middle of these details about my rape, the female minister said, "I'm getting a beep. I'm sorry; it hurts to remember. Can I call you back? I must take this call." It has been many years now, and I have yet to hear back from her.

Until the day I woke up in the hospital, I thought

The Strength of My Soul

God had forgotten about me. I had given up on life, but He never gave up on me. In my attempt to take my life, God assured me in that psychiatric ward that my life was too precious to take. If the suicide attempt had been successful, I would have not known how special I am to God. That day, so many years ago, almost broke me, but God said no.

Ava Cary is a singer, songwriter, and author who resides in Atlanta, Georgia. Ms. Cary received a full basketball scholarship at Norfolk State University (NSU), where she studied music. Originally from Owensboro, Kentucky, Ava found her gift in song at a young age in the church. She has performed for both religious and secular audiences across the country, who have been captivated and inspired by her strong and powerful voice. In 1976, Ava was crowned Miss Black Expo Princess. Later she was selected to perform with Kentucky's most competitive chorus, Mae Armi Chorus. She was the second African-American to receive the Mae Armi Award in the state of Kentucky. Ava has also made numerous appearances on the popular television show "Showtime at the Apollo" in New York. In 1998, Ava was asked to open up for one of her childhood influences, Shirley Caesar, during an appearance in Portsmouth, Virginia. She has also been invited to sing the National Anthem during many political and professional sporting events throughout the Southeast.

Ava is determined to use her gift of song to bless the world. She believes that God has gifted her with the ability to heal others through song. Ms. Cary is the mother of three beautiful young adults, Vince, Martell, and Quai, who are the pride of her life. Currently, she is working on her personal life story, *I'm So Sorry it Hurts to Remember*. In 2006, she released her first CD titled, "Ava Cary," and she is now working on her second CD, "Butterflies of Love," with the single release, "Love Almost Broke Me." Ava still keeps her priorities in order: God, family, and career. She can be contacted through her website, www.AvaSongstress.com, or through email at CaryAvawithyou@aol.com.

SOME GIFTS COME IN UGLY WRAPPING PAPER

Dawn Westmoreland

Lying in bed in a mental hospital for three days was the lowest I have ever felt in my life. I ended up in the mental health ward of the Charles George Veterans Affairs Medical Center in Asheville, North Carolina, after receiving horrific bullying and retaliation for blowing the whistle on the Midatlantic Consolidated Patient Accounting Center (MACPAC), which is a Veterans' Affairs agency. While I was not suicidal in the least, I was rundown and utterly exhausted. My psychiatrist highly recommended that I spend some time in this facility so I could rest and receive the medical care I needed.

The day I was admitted was my mother's birthday,

and I knew she would see the hospital identification on her caller ID when I called that day. There was no getting away from the fact that I was in the mental health ward. The staff even took care to take away my shoestrings and any sharp objects. It may have been part of the protocol, but it was still embarrassing, especially because I had once worked at this facility and knew some of the staff members. Of course, they pretended not to recognize me.

Sometimes we have to hit rock bottom so we can "see the light" and take positive action to align with our true purpose. From this perspective, landing in the mental health ward was a "gift" in ugly wrapping paper. I came to realize that I had become my own worst enemy by thinking I was a victim. Yes, life was not easy during this time, but it was made even more difficult because I bought into the idea that I *was* a victim. I had let my victimhood define me.

My Story

I began working for MACPAC in 2011. My depression, combined with physical injuries I had sustained while in the Air Force, classified me as a severely disabled military veteran (eighty percent disabled). I suffered from depression, migraines, neck, and shoulder issues, all of which were service related. I had worked in the Human Resources department at the Charles George Veterans Affairs Medical Center for two years before transferring to MACPAC, where I then began an administrative position that involved spending most of my time on a computer. Having spent twenty-two years in human resources, including five years of work at the Veteran Affairs, I was very familiar with the laws that affect and govern human resources within a government agency. Perhaps, then, you can imagine my surprise when I observed within weeks what appeared to be nepotism within the MACPAC hiring structure.

Some of the management's family and friends were being offered promotions, while more highly trained and educated employees remained at the bottom of the career scale. In addition, certain family and friends of management were offered training that would later qualify only them for a position. This deeply disturbed me. From my years of experience in the field and the masters degree I had received in Management/HR, among other degrees, I could clearly see that these individuals were getting preferential treatment. This really angered me, since I knew it was very wrong! It is illegal for a government agency to hire family and friends while in a management role, yet they had done so and were actively creating circumstances that promoted those same people.

There is a problem with veteran homelessness; so many vets want to be hired by Veteran Affairs for the benefits and to feel more secure, but they often can't even get into the system because of nepotism. A veteran who lost his or her legs, for example, could really benefit from an administrative position with Veterans Affairs, but only if he or she can get in! Unfair hiring of family and friends is more than wrong, it's illegal. And it will only stop when the leadership ceases the practice and holds people accountable for their actions.

Bound by my responsibility to uphold the law, and driven by my level of integrity, I pressed charges against MACPAC through the Office of Special Counsel and later to the Equal Employment Opportunity Commission. After I filed the charges, MACPAC management quite suddenly began finding fault with my work. Given my history in HR and my knowledge of and education in the field, I knew that they could not sanction disciplinary action against me for anything not officially listed as a performance standard in my employee performance plan. And yet the management staff wrote me up for all kinds of performance issues that were not specific to my performance plan, even going so far as to file charges within Veteran Affairs against me for supposed violations, such as Absence Without Leave (AWOL), a security violation, and other related charges.

My saving grace was that I learned many years ago to document everything. Knowing that my work emails were being monitored, I began a daily practice of printing out physical copies of non-private documentation. Later, having this documentation of correspondence with MACPAC management would make my employment attorney's job much easier. Within the emails, I had cited to MACPAC officials the proper US codes, manuals, and regulations the agency was violating. I highly recommend that anyone bullied in the workplace make an effort to keep very good records.

Workplace Bullying

Many of the MACPAC employees were family and friends of management, so I knew much of the staff was watching my every move. I received many angry looks and overheard other staff members speaking ill of me. I was even cautioned by a concerned friend to keep a close eye on the food and drinks I put in one of the refrigerators at work.

As a retired member of the United States Air Force, who had previously held many leadership positions, I turned my focus to being a good worker and tried to ignore the negative behaviors that were aimed at me. I worked hard not to get sucked into the drama or negativity, but the harassment got so intense that my mental, emotional, and physical health began to suffer. In fact, I used to get very sick every Sunday evening, knowing that I had to work at a hostile workplace the next day. Not fun! Also, within the laws for medically necessary reasonable accommodation, I asked for an adjusted workspace so I could sit without pain and the risk of further injury, since my position required more than six hours a day at my computer. A physical therapist was eventually granted to come and make the required ergonomic changes to my working area, but many of the implementations were delayed for months, during which I spent many hours undergoing physical therapy for the pain my work environment had caused.

It appeared as though the MACPAC management was actively blocking the workplace adjustments I so desperately needed. It felt like I was being punished. In addition, against my doctor's orders, my management would not allow me to work at home as a medical reasonable accommodation (RA). To my dismay, I later found out that another employee had been allowed to work at home, and upon communicating with this employee, found out that we had both properly filed for a medical RA.

That's when my psychiatrist recommended a stay at the Charles George Veterans Affairs Medical Center. On her advice, I took an official leave of absence to receive medical care. MACPAC management then seized that opportunity to file false Absence Without Leave (AWOL) charges against me.

They had gone too far. I pressed charges against MACPAC with the Equal Employment Opportunity Commission (EEOC) for disability discrimination. Then, I filed further charges for the ongoing retaliatory workplace bullying and harassment. The EEOC Administrative Judge later combined the two cases. MACPAC management had me "temporarily removed" from my job for nearly 100 days, while I still received pay while the Veteran Affairs lawyers made their legal review of the many false charges the agency had leveled against me.

I ended up in a leave-without-pay status. I was living in a very nice house at the time, but in a matter of months I could not pay my bills, resulting in delinquency. My credit score and financial portrait were compromised. I take those responsibilities very seriously, so this was quite frankly the saddest time of my life. Feeling this low, and being concerned for my safety, put my mental and physical health in serious decline. I dealt with most of my ordeal alone, since my family lived in other states. They supported me as much they could, but still I felt alone.

Finding Resolution

Many people who are bullied at work don't have the training to understand how to defend themselves. Luckily, I had twenty-two years of experience in human resources and several degrees in HR and management to provide me with the tools I needed. I found an employment attorney in Asheville, North Carolina, who was compassionate, smart, and willing to work with my financial situation.

I will never forget when we deposed two of the

top management officials. Bullies that are deposed or ousted by an attorney have a whole different demeanor than when they're in bully mode. I actually felt sorry for them, but I also wanted them to be held accountable for their actions.

EEOC cases are triaged based on severity of the case. Due to the severe retaliation and bullying I received for being a Veteran Affairs "whistleblower," my case was deemed "severe" and I received an EEOC hearing within a year by the EEOC Administrative Judge in Charlotte, North Carolina. By the time I was granted my hearing, I was suffering from leaky gut syndrome, depression, anxiety, and a variety of other painful physical issues. Putting one foot in front of the other was exhausting, and I could barely recognize my reflection in the mirror. My skin even turned yellow! Stress can severely harm you.

Two days before the EEOC Administrative hearing, the Veterans Affairs and I resolved the matter. I won an emotional victory! I refused to sign a "gag order," which would have prevented me from talking about my cases, and to my knowledge, no VA managers were held accountable for their actions. Occasionally, I receive phone calls from current employees in the MACPAC who tell me the work environment has not improved. Well, I hope that in sharing my story, I can help others who are facing similar challenges.

I did my best to find all the healthy balance I could in my life, but as I mentioned at the beginning of this chapter, I was stuck in my role as a victim. And this mentality did not empower me to break free. Instead, I had to recognize my success and allow myself to let go of my victimhood and embrace my personal power. When I was finally able to do this, I realized that this was at the heart of my ongoing work with others. I had gone through the "dark days of the soul" to become empowered.

Empowering "Leaders in Hiding"

I realized that I was the perfect person to go through my ordeal! You could say I had an epiphany in March 2013, when I had spent three days in the mental health from the stress of being bullied. Once I realized my calling, it was time to step fully into my empowerment so I could help others do the same. Through speaking, coaching, writing, interviewing, and consulting with people who are sick and tired of feeling stressed out, overwhelmed, and attacked, I have made it my mission to empower these "leaders in hiding."

If you are ready to change the way you look at things and are open to making a positive shift in your life, it is no coincidence that you are reading my story right now. My heart goes out to you. I have learned how to transform my life and have refined the techniques to help you realize your dreams and even faster than I did, as long you are willing to do the work and are open to suggestions. Get ready to be empowered!

Five Tips for the Bullied or Dis-Empowered

First, you must love and respect yourself. If you believe in yourself, you will project powerful attributes to other people. Your presence and your demeanor tell everyone how you feel about yourself. If you carry yourself with dignity and grace, others will perceive you that way. Bullies, who generally have low self-esteem, can pick up your energy and know that you may be an easy target to harass. Generally, they go after the people they deem as weak. Work with a coach, mentor, religious clergyman or clergywoman, or whoever can help you become more empowered.

Second, manage and maintain documentation. I cannot stress enough that if you are being bullied at work, having great documentation is so important to helping you get a fair outcome. If you do not have good documentation, you may have a hard time winning in court or getting a fair settlement. Be sure to hand-carry your documentation home. Do not email it, since it can be monitored.

Third, conquer your hurtful past and heal! When you heal, you cease to attract negative circumstances. Get professional help. You cannot emotionally, psychologically, or financially afford to carry on with negativity.

Fourth, cultivate positive thoughts and actions. This involves choosing our thoughts and actions wisely. More often than most of us realize, *we* create the unwanted drama in our lives.

Fifth, quit the blame game! Stop blaming others or thinking they can control you. Once you do this, you will become "unstuck" and be able to take charge of your life. Give yourself permission to let go of your old stories and make healthy life changes.

My story has a positive ending. I realized that I had been given gifts in ugly wrapping paper, which helped me to become the woman I am today—a personal power coach. I began a one-year training program as a coach, one week after I settled with the Veteran Affairs. I now help women find their voice, strength, and personal power.

In April of 2015, I was contracted and compensated to go to Washington DC to educate senators on the need for protecting whistleblowers like myself. The Christian Science Monitor even commended me in an article for the work I am doing to empower others today, assisting other whistleblowers in different industries and others who feel dis-empowered to understand their rights, protection, and ways to find calm throughout their ordeals. Now, laws are being passed in the senate to help people like me who are willing to turn in those who act badly and break the law. So, be sure to share your goals and wishes with God because amazing things can happen!

In her book, *The Empowered Whistleblower: A Practical and Spiritual Path to Personal Power*, **Dawn Westmoreland** shares her story of overcoming her own dis-empowerment. In life, even negative experiences can be a gift in ugly wrapping paper as long as you find the lesson or growth in each one. Throughout her life, Dawn has blown the "whistle" on disempowerment in many forms and is now teaching others, as a speaker, author, coach, and hypnotherapist, how to step up and break the chains that keep them from attaining their personal power.

Dawn has been featured in numerous radio and magazine interviews, where she has shared empowerment strategies with those who want more joy and fulfillment in their lives. Dawn Marie Westmoreland has been lauded by the Christian Science Monitor for her work to empower others and alert the federal government to her managers' actions at the VA she once worked at, alleging favoritism for hiring and training that advanced only a select few.

You can learn more about Dawn at:
www.DawnMarieWestmoreland.com.

FACE IT, OR IT WILL FOLLOW YOU

SharRon Jamison

When I was growing up, I was constantly bullied. I was awkward and shy, and I was really ill equipped emotionally to handle being the only Black girl in a newly integrated classroom. I was different—too different—and since I had no friends or allies, I became the target of tormentors. Yes, unfortunately, I became the focus and victim of their verbal and physical abuse. And boy, did I suffer. I endured more insults and absorbed more body blows than you can imagine. The boys were relentless, and my cries for mercy did nothing to stop their physical attacks on my body and their verbal assaults on my soul.

Most days, I was kicked, called names, and spat on. And after every assault, I lost more confidence in my ability to protect myself. I became more terrified, so terrified that I didn't even fight back. I wanted to defend myself, but I was so scared that I could not raise my fist to throw a punch, even though my brain instructed me to do so. And what was most unfortunate was that I was a big girl who had the girth and power to deliver a good uppercut. I outweighed the boys by more than forty pounds, and I was very athletic. But even though I was physically bigger, taller, and stronger, I was so intimidated I failed to muster enough strength and confidence to fight back. The adage is true: take the will; win the fight. The kids had decimated my spirit. They took my will. And as a result, they won every fight.

My reluctance to defend myself created a vicious cycle of abuse that continued for months. Since I would not or could not protect myself, the bullies became more emboldened. And as their confidence grew, more bullies joined in. As the number of bullies increased, the number of hits, shoves, taunts, and punches that I endured increased significantly. It was a nightmare that seemed to have no end in sight.

I suffered, and every day grew more intimidated—truly petrified. I prayed for the hitting to stop, because at that time, the pommels hurt more than the words. As an adult, I now know that words are just as damaging, but at nine years old, I had no way of knowing that. All I wanted was for the blows to my body to stop; I was weary of the torture. So I tried everything that my young mind could think of to stop or delay the almost daily battles. But despite my attempts to make peace, plead for mercy, or purchase my safety, the cycle continued for months. Trust me, I begged the boys to stop. I offered my lunch, I offered to do homework, and I offered to steal candy, anything for a truce. But nothing satisfied their insatiable desire to humiliate me. To them, I was not a classmate; I was a punching bag without emotions, feelings, or pain. I was a toy, an object, the focus of their homebred bigotry. I was many things, but what they didn't see was that I was a human being, a little girl and a scared child.

But one day, I had enough, and I turned around and faced the bullies, no longer willing to absorb the kicks to my legs, shoves in my back, and the punches in my stomach. I was tired of being embarrassed and degraded, and honestly, I was tired of being scared. So one day, when a little boy kicked me, I turned around beat the crap out of him. I kicked, punched, bit, and yelled. I am not sure if it was fear or fury, but I fought until I was drained, tired, and sweaty. Even though I was outnumbered, I faced the bullies. I am not sure if I won the fight, but I did win their respect. And thankfully—finally—they left me alone.

On that day, I learned an important lesson that changed my life. I learned that if I faced my bullies, they wouldn't follow me. Even though I could not articulate everything I felt, I somehow knew that something in my spirit had shifted. I was no longer afraid, and most of all, I no longer felt powerless. I faced the spineless little jerks, and because I did, they no longer had the guts to follow me. No more chasing, no more stalking, no more hunting, no more hitting, and no more fear. That realization changed my life.

Over the years, I have learned that unresolved pain can be a bully. Just like my hellish classmates who followed me, unsettled and unacknowledged pain will follow you if you don't face it. I don't care how hard you try to dodge the memories, camouflage the spiritual injuries, evade the physical ailments, or suppress the thoughts—if you fail to face your pain, it will tempt you, track you, and test you. You can chant all night, pray all morning, and quote affirmations for lunch, but your pain will demand your attention. Maybe it won't every day, but it will surface, and at the most inopportune times.

Even if you attempt to hide your pain in liquor, numb your pain with drugs, anesthetize your pain with food, freeze your pain with sex, or dull your pain with work, if not addressed, your pain will visit you when your defenses are down, when you are emotionally vulnerable, and when you are alone. You may not care to acknowledge your pain, but it will lurk, linger, and meander until you effectively deal with it. It will influence your choices, dictate your decisions, inform your thinking, and affect your behavior. Your pain will also manipulate you, coerce you, boss you around, limit you, and confuse you. Even when you refuse to talk about it, your pain will demand to be seen, heard, and felt; it will not be denied.

Face your pain. If it is too great, start by gradually peeling back the layers just enough to see what's driving your despair and negating your power. Face the demons that haunt you, face the memories that shame you, and face the lies that demean you. Don't let pain steal your inner peace. Don't let your inner demons harass you. Don't let your insecurities torment you. Don't let secrets terrorize you. Don't let old guilt oppress you. Don't let past mistakes limit you. And don't let old addictions and habits persecute you. Expose your pain. Write about it, talk about it, and process it. Face it even if you have to face it with tears in your eyes.

I learned that bullies are not so tough when they realize you are strong, fearless, and resolute. Trust me, bullies understand that most of their power is based on threats and intimidation, not follow-through. The same can be said about your pain. When your pain realizes that you have the power to recognize it, address it, control it, and channel it, it will lose its power over your life. It will diminish, and the real, powerful you will be set free.

A wise woman once told me that if you don't deal with your pain, your pain would deal with you. So deal with your pain. Don't try to hide from it, and don't mask it. Most of all, don't try to jump or leap over your pain to get to a place called "fine," "I got this," or "I'm okay." Arrival at those places takes time, intention, and loving support.

Always remember that healing is not a sprint; it is a walk, and sometimes it is a slow one. But it is a process that is uniquely yours. Healing is not instantaneous; it is incremental. It is not continuous

The Strength of My Soul

either; healing is full of starts and stops. It is a journey, and every step of your healing journey is important.

I still remember the relief I felt when I faced my foes. Even now, as I recall that moment, I feel a warm rushing sensation in my spirit that touches the very core of my soul. When I faced my foes, I was free! I was finally able to walk home in peace without being pursued. No more running, no more panting, and no more protecting my face from fists. No more wiping spit off my face or off my coat. No more brushing dirt off my clothes or picking up my lunch box from the ground. No more begging and pleading for mercy. No more crying as I tried to find my pencils, papers, and crayons that were scattered on the sidewalk. No more torn-up homework and dirty shoes. No more! I was free.

Face your pain so it will not follow you. Pain hurts, and healing hurts, too, but you can do it. Remember that pain, like bullies, has only the power you give it. So take your power back. Face your pain, and get free once and for all. I promise you that when you face it, it will not follow you. I know you can do it. Blessings!

—Adapted from *I Have Learned A Few Things*

SharRon Jamison, MBA, is an inspirational speaker, minister, life strategist, entrepreneur, and author. For over twenty-five years, she has passionately encouraged people to transform their lives physically, emotionally, and spiritually. From her initial work as a personal trainer and owner of Fitness F'ness to her work as a licensed minister, she has motivated people to love, honor, and appreciate who they are and to embrace all that they can be.

SharRon earned a Bachelor of Arts from Hampton University in Hampton, Virginia. She earned a Masters of Business Administration from Nova Southeastern University, and is currently pursuing her Master of Divinity at the Interdenominational Theological Center in Atlanta, Georgia.

In addition, SharRon is the Founder/CEO of The Jamison Group, a company committed to providing leadership, diversity, and empowerment workshops and training to individuals, groups, businesses, and faith-based organizations. She is also an account manager with an international biotechnology firm and has over twenty-five successful years in the biopharmaceutical industry. SharRon is a passionate speaker, seasoned facilitator, an empathetic life coach, a business professional, a certified personal trainer, a licensed minister, a proud mother, and the author of two books, *I Can Depend on Me* and *I Have Learned A Few Things*. Her new book, *50 Choices To A Fulfilling Life* will be released in late 2015. *The Strength of My Soul: Stories of Sisterhood, Triumph and Inspiration* is her first anthology project.

Love & Loss

ANCHORED IN LOVE

Brandy Jenkins and Nikki Rashan

"Few words can describe the range of emotions that spun inside of me after I heard four confirming words from a doctor I had met only days prior. 'You have breast cancer,' he told me over the phone. It was only a couple of days prior that this stranger performed a biopsy on me, then stating, "I'm pretty sure it's cancer." Confirmation was another thing. At that time I didn't know what the future held, only that it was going to be drastically different than I had envisioned for myself." - Author Nikki Rashan

On October 1, 2013, my life as I knew it was forever changed. That day marked the beginning of a journey to demonstrate, as fervently as possible, my vows to my lovely wife, Nikki Rashan; I will love you in the good days and love you more than enough in the not-so-good days. The afternoon Nikki found out about her cancer, I called her from work while on my lunch break to ask if she had heard from the doctor. Casually, Nikki said she had and began to share with me what she had learned. With my ear pressed firmly against my cell phone, I listened intently as she confirmed my greatest fear: "Well babe, he says it's cancer." My heart felt as if it had been punctured with a sharp object. I felt a nervous energy inside of me slowly build with every word she spoke. As I listened, my breathing became short and fast. The office lobby I was in appeared foggy, and though I saw people talking, I heard nothing but Nikki's voice. I had no words. After every sentence I simply said, "mm-hmm." I was angry. I was mad. I was downright devastated. After having lost to cancer my father in 2011 and my mother in 2012, I thought this was a cruel joke. My feelings were hurt.

After we said we loved each other and would see each other soon, I rose to my feet, grabbed the tuna salad I had purchased for lunch, walked across the lobby to enter the elevator to return to the twenty-first floor, placed my salad in the trash, entered the restroom, locked the last stall, and wept. I wept for my wife, the mother of two beautiful daughters, a sister, a daughter, an aunt, a wonderful friend to many. How did this happen? How did we get here? Are they sure? What does this mean? These were just some of the questions that crowded my mind. That Tuesday afternoon awakened an emotion that I still feel burning inside me.

She had her first chemotherapy session on October 28, 2013. Nikki was aware of my dislike for needles, blood, and anything gruesome, but she said, "It's not about you, babe. Show her that you're here with her in every moment." I watched as they connected the lines for transfusion. I sucked in the air through my nose and exhaled it through my mouth, hoping to control my tears. Twirling my wedding band on my left ring finger, I sat with shaking knees. I didn't know what to expect. We looked at each other, smiled, and allowed our tears to fall. This was just the beginning. Through it all, I would love her passionately.

Being present is essential to advocating for a loved one. Though my heart wanted to check out and not accept our harsh reality, I could not allow fear to overrule my love for her. More than ever, she needed me. More than ever I wanted her to rest in my love and trust that I would be exactly what she needed. I had to show up day after day to provide strength, support, courage, and a smiling face in the midst of cloudy days.

The treatment plan consisted of sixteen rounds of chemotherapy, a double mastectomy with immediate reconstruction, and twenty-five rounds of radiation. Through the entire plan, my wife gracefully braved it all. Never did she complain. She embraced her beautiful bald head, her weight loss, and her nails and her breasts, discolored from treatment and radiation. She took those issues with stride because soon it would be over. April 15, 2014, was the last day of chemo. May 27, 2014, was her double mastectomy with immediate reconstruction. Radiation would begin July 28, 2014. Five days a week for five weeks, Nikki knocked out the radiation. And soon we began to see the light at the end of the tunnel. Our hearts were filled with joy! Of course, there were a few days she didn't feel well, but we expected that after the ordeal she had experienced over the past ten months. Our focus was on preparing ourselves for the celebration.

In Nikki's words, *"Just before radiation began, I noticed a small bump in the bend of my right arm. I didn't concern myself with it. With all I had been through and being aware of potential issues I could have with my right arm, I cast any concern aside.*

Well, a second one popped up a couple weeks later. Then a third and fourth, all in random areas of my upper body. I reached out to my primary doctor and was told to see my oncologist. I was in my second to last week of radiation when I met with an oncologist after radiation. It was then that I knew. He didn't say anything other than the lumps needed a biopsy. But it was the look on his face ... I read the results in his bleak expression. I hadn't made it out of the building before bursting in tears. I cried a lot that day. The following week I had the biopsy and on the afternoon of Friday, August 29th, shortly after completing my final round of radiation that morning, I learned that the lumps (subcutaneous nodules) were cancerous. Talk about a blow ... I was devastated."

– Author Nikki Rashan, from *Pray or Worry, Don't Do Both*, www.nikkiandbrandy.blogspot.com

On August 29th, Nikki's friend Benita accompanied her to an appointment for a check-up. It wasn't often that we allowed her to go alone. I texted them both throughout the appointment to ask how things were going and what the doctors were saying. In the beginning the responses came from

Nikki. Then Benita answered. But suddenly, the texts stopped, and when I later received a response, it was short, unlike the ones before it. I could feel my heart pounding harder and harder. I began to rationalize why they weren't responding and why the responses weren't as detailed as before. "Oh, Brandy you know the reception isn't good in the hospital. And you know Benita is probably trying to listen to everything the doctor is saying to give you a report." Yeah, that sounds about right. I would question and answer myself. I texted Benita, "I'll be getting off soon, should I come up to the hospital? I can have someone drop me off up there." Her response was simply, "yes." I stared at my screen for the longest time. Why did she say yes? Nikki had our car, but a co-worker was headed that way, so I got a ride with her.

Nikki was my greatest protector. It was her protection that made Benita not tell me what was going on. The car ride was approximately twenty minutes. The entire ride, I prayed for good news. My heart wouldn't allow me to think anything else. I just wanted to get to Nikki. I needed to see her. When I arrived, I got out and walked as fast as I could. It was almost as if I was run-walking. Even waiting on the elevator ride to the fourth floor seemed to take forever. As I exited the elevator, I looked to my right, then to my left, and there were Nikki and Benita standing by the window. I smiled and locked eyes with Nikki, but she quickly turned away. I'm sure my facial expression showed concern. Then I looked at Benita, who shook her head and started to cry. "Hey, babe," I said. "What's going on? What's up?" I hugged Nikki while Benita updated me on the news. I recall feeling numb, violent, and disoriented at the same time. I couldn't stop moving. Nikki and I hugged for a long-short time while standing in the hall. I was in total shock. I needed to see her doctor. I needed to use the restroom. I needed my momma. I needed my daddy. I needed God to tell me something.

Many days we cried and held each other in silence. Our tears did not compromise our strength. During those moments, our souls continued to cultivate the connection we had had with one another. Our eighteen-month journey with breast cancer was a life-changing event. The level of intimacy we developed was nothing I could ever have imagined. To this day, our connection and bond is unbreakable. It was my pleasure to love Nikki so unconditionally. I knew no other way. Seeing her smile was my reward. Everything about loving her made me feel good. Love—real love—demands self-sacrifice. Nikki taught me that it isn't about you—it's about being present for the other person and fulfilling her needs.

On May 4, 2015, Nikki was granted her eternal wings. I am grateful to have experienced her love, which will surely sustain me for the rest of my life. To have witnessed the strength of a woman who at every turn faced disappointed and still managed to smile, stand tall, and keep going. In turn, this gives me strength. Despite my tears, my lonely nights, and my heartache even now, I am inspired. She was indeed my earth angel, now watching over our children and me from heaven.

Nikki's journey taught me the substance of faith. Sometimes I had witnessed things that weakened me. However, what I felt brewing on the inside, permeating its presence within my spirit, kept me locked into my promise to love her in sickness and in health. God never said it would be easy, but He did promise to provide strength during the storm. I was entrusted with the care of my beautiful wife, and I believed I was given everything I needed to walk this journey with her. What I knew was that I had to dig deep and be Nikki's anchor. I did my best to keep her encouraged despite my pain and my fear. As long as we remained planted in the goodness and mercy of our God, all will be well.

Allow me to provide some background about us. We met the summer of 2002 and fell into a swift, comfortable, and gentle friendship. To describe the manner in which we met cannot be left to just a paragraph. Many say this, and we will as well: our union was 110 percent destiny. The night we met, a greater force touched and brought us together. We remained friends, though miles apart, after I had moved to another state the year after we met. In 2009, after years of supporting one another through life's ups and downs, we took our friendship to another level, to a place that far exceeds what either of us had imagined love to be. We committed our love on July 14, 2012, in an intimate ceremony in San Juan, Puerto Rico. We were legally married July 14, 2013, in Studio City, California. We have three daughters whom we love dearly. **Brandy Nasha** resides in Los Angeles, CA

The late **Nikki Rashan** published four novels: *Double Pleasure, Double Pain; You Make Me Wanna; Cyber Case;* and *The Exchange*. In addition, she published two novellas: *Carl Weber's Full Figured Series: Sugar on the Side* and *Les Tales: Tempted to*

The Strength of My Soul

Touch, which was part of a collaboration.

Nikki Rashan Jenkins – Rest In Love.
August 18, 1972 – May 4, 2015

Blog: www.nikkiandbrandy.blogspot.com
Email: nikkiandbrandy@gmail.com
Phone: (414) 687-1446

A BIG FISH AND A LITTLE RED BIRD
Nicole Varner

A story about loss and grace

Here in the South we have a strong tradition of storytelling and tall tales. We even have a name for this. We call it a "big fish." As I reflect on the subject of loss, I feel compelled to share my own "big fish" about death, loss, and coming to peace with it. Some people might find my story a bit mysterious, even metaphysical but, unlike that strong Southern tradition of the big fish, it is not exaggerated; it is my truth.

One summer night, when I was around fourteen or fifteen, I dreamt that both my parents, who had divorced when I was seven, died at the same time. I woke up in tears, shattered by the details of the dream. My father would die before my mother and would be found dead in his home by my aunt Mary Alice, whom I adored. I sat up in bed and struggled to compose myself. Without telling my dad about this dream, I got dressed and went across the street to uncle Frank and aunt Mary Alice's house, where the comfort of seeing them and playing with my cousins awaited.

Now, you may be thinking, "Well, maybe that dream was just coincidental, and besides, that's not really a stretch because statistically women live longer than men." But here's where, for me, it became mysterious and mystical: I only had that dream once, and it was so vivid that it stayed with me, haunting me for years to the point where I really began to believe that my father would die first and then my mother. I was reluctant to tell anyone about it, out of fear that speaking it would make it come true.

In September of 2004, I recalled this dream as I sat between my sister Diana and my partner, Tiffany, on the front pew of the church, staring at my father in his casket. I felt lost, deeply lonely, sitting there without my parents, who were the bedrock of my life. Beneath my breath, I continually repeated, "God's grace is sufficient, God's grace is sufficient." Diana and Tiffany heard me and joined in. Tiffany held my hand and tried to console me, even though she was traveling on her own journey of loss.

Just eighteen months earlier, Tiffany and I went to her hometown of Akron, Ohio, to bury her stepfather, who had died of cancer. Her mother entrusted the two of us with the task of reviewing and approving his body for presentation. She had held his hand as he transitioned, and only wanted to remember him as she last saw him, looking up at her with a smile on his face.

So there we were at the funeral home in the middle of the day, going in to see Tiffany's stepfather. Outside, the sun was shining bright. Yet inside the chapel where he lay in state, it was dark except for a single spotlight shining on him. I remember thinking how lonely it felt in the room. I held Tiffany's hand tightly as the two of us approached his casket. This was the first time I had ever had to console someone I loved romantically during a major loss, and I felt inadequate. How do you console someone who is facing the inconsolable? Tiffany was very strong about it. She didn't cry, and she didn't break down. So I stayed strong, too, and governed my reactions according to her actions.

The Strength of My Soul

We left Akron and went back to Atlanta to begin to heal as best we could. We went back to work with our game faces on, glossing over the truth we all dare not utter aloud—that there is nothing anyone could say or do to make our loss acceptable. While we could appreciate and cherish the words and actions of love, encouragement, and sympathy, when we were alone, we truly felt the void and the pain of loss.

About a year after we said goodbye to Tiffany's stepfather, my mother was diagnosed with stomach cancer. She underwent chemotherapy and surgery to remove the tumor from her stomach. Despite these life-saving efforts, the cancer eventually spread to her lungs and she was diagnosed as terminal. The doctors estimated that my mom had a few months to live. Once I had a chance to step away from the flurry of decisions about my mother's medical care, I again thought of the dream I had as a teenager, and this new scenario confused me, because it seemed out of sync with the dream. I decided it was time to share that dream with someone. So I told Tiffany about it, and about how it had led me to believe my father would die first and that my aunt Mary Alice would find him on the floor of his kitchen. But I never mentioned that dream to my father.

I had yet to tell my father that my mother was dying. I knew I had to tell him because she was in the ICU and the end would soon come. But I couldn't quite find the words. One morning, for some strange reason, I couldn't seem to get out the house for work as efficiently as I usually did. My father, who loved to garden, would often bring a basket of vegetables harvested from his garden and leave it on our front porch. That particular morning, I happened to walk past the front door as he was leaving his goodie basket. I saw him and invited him inside. He sat down on the sofa. I sat across from him on the edge of our coffee table and said, "Dad, I need to tell you something about Mom." He looked at me intently, and I could barely speak while my eyes filled with tears. I told him, "Mom is in ICU and they've only given her a few more weeks." I looked up at him and he looked away, as if he just couldn't bear to see me so sad. But he dismissed the notion that anyone knows how much time someone might have to live. "Nikki," he said, "only the good Lawd knows."

My father always knew how to comfort me. When I was twelve and my maternal grandfather died, my father saw me crying as we left the church after her funeral. He rushed toward me seemingly from nowhere to hug and protect me. In that moment, talking to him as an adult about the pending loss of my mother, I thought to myself, "Mom has to move on to a new realm, but me and Dad, we'll have each other in this realm for some time more."

Never would I have guessed that it would be last time I ever saw my father alive.

Nearly two weeks later, early on a Sunday morning, I was dreaming again. I was in a white room with my back against the wall. I heard a non-gendered, omnidirectional voice say, "She's dead." Then another voice chimed in, "No, it's the other one." I woke up with a feeling of dread, a sense that someone, possibly my father, was gone. Just like I did when I had had that dream as a teenager, I pushed it aside, got dressed, and went about starting my day. The intellectual and spiritual parts of myself began to debate. My intellectual side said I was being paranoid and irrational; my spiritual side said that indisputably my scary dream had just come true. I decided to call my father and prove just how ridiculous I was being. But I didn't call right away. I put it off until the afternoon because I was being a coward, like we all are when we don't want to face reality. The truth is that in moments like this, no matter how we try to hide from and dismiss the reality of life, reality knows exactly where we are and how to find us because at some point we have to reckon with it.

The call to Dad never happened. Before I could dial his number that afternoon, I received a call from the Clayton County Police Department. Tiffany and I had just left a gathering at a co-worker's house to watch the Atlanta Falcons game, and I was driving back home. The officer asked if I had spoken to my mother that day. I told him I hadn't, and that my mother was in ICU, dying. The officer asked me to come to my dad's house in Clayton County, because my aunt had found him dead in his kitchen. I went numb. It's such an odd feeling to be acutely aware that you have no feelings. "Pull over," Tiffany said. So I did. She took the wheel and drove us the rest of the way to my dad's house. We pulled up to see Uncle Frank and many of my cousins standing outside waiting for me. The officers on the scene wanted me to go inside and see my father, since I was his next of kin. But I opted not to; I gave permission for my Uncle Alonzo and a couple cousins to go inside instead. I called our family's preferred funeral home and held my Uncle Frank's hand until they came to remove my father's body. Uncle Alonzo came out and handed me my father's wallet. I still have it to this day.

The night of my father's wake, my sister, Tiffany, and I went to the hospital to see my mom. My mother was an evangelist, and one of the most honest people I've ever known. I always admired her strength and her unfaltering dedication. Although she and I differed when it came to certain points of our respective religious beliefs, I respected the fact that she did exactly what she said she believed, and she always did it in a spirit of love. In her retirement, my mother dedicated her time and her savings to establishing a mission in an economically challenged neighborhood to give children hope through the belief in something greater than themselves. I consider myself more of a progressive Christian; I believe there is space for science and all of that. Mom, however, was more traditional. Very Pentecostal. And very spiritually perceptive. She grew even more so during her illness. She was aware of the gravity of the situation I was in, not only about the loss of my dad but the impending loss of her, too. Although she was heavily sedated when we visited after Dad's wake, Mom responded when my sister asked her to open her eyes. She looked directly at me, and I knew in that moment that I didn't need to tell her about Dad. I sensed that she already knew.

Within a matter of days, my mother made her transition, too. The day it happened, my sister came to break the news. Later on, I found myself at another funeral home with Tiffany. My sister and some other relatives were there as well. I looked up at the sky above the funeral home, and saw a double rainbow appear. Now, I understand the science of how rainbows are created, but I had never seen a double rainbow before. And so far, I haven't seen another one. That double rainbow was seemingly there waiting on us, and within five minutes it disappeared. In Christianity, rainbows signify God's faithfulness and mercy. A double rainbow is also said to symbolize a transition in life. To me, that double rainbow was a symbol of hope. I felt it was put there to let me know that my parents were okay.

After both funerals, Tiffany and I tried to close this two-year chapter of parental loss and return to our normal lives. We didn't have children, but we did have Ozzie, our Chinese crested. Ozzie was our fur-baby, our family, and we loved, nurtured, and protected him as if he were still a puppy, even though he was about two years old.

The Strength of My Soul

Suddenly, within two weeks of my mom's burial, Ozzie suffered a seizure. That was too much for me. Tiffany rushed Ozzie to the vet, but he died. We lost our fourth family member and reached our tipping point. All the agony and pain from two years of losses leveled us. We screamed in pain and cried together: Really, the dog, too? We stayed in the house the entire weekend, crying.

When I was growing up, my father and I would go to a small nondescript diner on Saturday mornings for breakfast. This diner looked like it had been a Waffle House previously. We'd sit at the counter, and Dad would give me a dollar in coins to put in the old jukebox, to play some of our favorite songs as we ate. First in rotation, always, was one of his favorites, "Another Somebody Done Somebody Wrong Song." I'd do my best country singer imitation and sing along, "Hey, could you play another somebody done somebody wrong song? And make me feel at home." With so many parents and our dear Ozzie gone, our reality was starting to get sadder than even that country song could convey. I took to crying in secret, mostly in the shower.

After many months of secret grief, one morning, while sleeping in a little later than usual, I had a dream that my mother was coming through the French doors located off our bedroom. In my dream, my mother approached my bedside to comfort me. She reached out to touch me with the consoling and loving hands only a mother would have. I was awakened simultaneously by Tiffany's touch. She was at the edge of the bed telling me that she was leaving for work. This, I was convinced, was my mother's way of spiritually connecting with me without frightening me. After that, I felt as if a huge burden had been lifted from me, and I no longer cried in the shower.

A few months passed and it was springtime. Again I was awakened from my sleep, this time by a beautiful red cardinal pecking at my window. We had lived in this house for almost two years at that point, and never before had such a thing occurred. At first, I thought, oh, that bird will go away, but it didn't. The cardinal came back every day and pecked at the window. My curiosity was piqued. One day, I walked through our living room much like I did the day my father dropped by with his gift of vegetables, and I told him about my mom's diagnosis. I noticed the cardinal was pecking at the window again, and I had to laugh to myself. I whispered conspiratorially to the bird, "Mom, is that you? Or is it you, Dad?"

Determined to make that cardinal go away, I went online and Googled "how to make a bird stop pecking at a window." I put some of our new dog's stuffed animals in the window in an attempt to scare it away. But, just like any of the challenges and things that frighten us, nothing would make that cardinal go away. He even brought along more cardinals. I finally acknowledged and embraced the red cardinal and his friends, and began leaving food for them. I came to find comfort in the fact that they had chosen our home. That was nine years ago, and every spring the cardinals' return. However, they have never pecked at the windows again.

The cardinals' red color is symbolic of faith and power; its cycle of twelve is also symbolic of life, death, and renewal. Every year, in case I've lost my way (as we humans do), lost my faith, lost my belief that there is something greater than me, lost my connection with the universe and to all living things, or somehow forgotten that we are all one energy—grace comes in the form of a vibrant red bird to remind me that in this life, we're all connected.

Science teaches us that energy is neither created nor is it destroyed. The unmerited grace which I receive every day when I awaken to this consciousness is what gives me the ability to celebrate and appreciate the now.

People often ask me how I've dealt with the losses—how *we've* dealt with the losses. Tiffany and I have dealt with the losses as best we can. We've grieved, since it is a part of the healing process. However, we must learn to live in the moment because all we have is the right now. If I've learned nothing else, it is profoundly apparent to me that when we transition, everything stops for us in that moment, in this world. From my perspective, people should become connected to the infinite possibilities of a limitless universe and the energy that surrounds us every day. Understand that each of us is on a unique journey, in this moment, and we don't know what the next part of our journey looks like. Nevertheless, we can find peace and happiness, knowing that if we open our hearts and minds, we will receive signs of grace that will comfort and heal our pains and allow us to fully enjoy the beautiful moments we have in this space and in this moment, because grace is sufficient.

Nicole Varner is a Georgia native. Raised and educated in the South, she has an appreciation for tradition, beauty, and roots. She is currently a Technical Project Manager for a large corporation and a freelance photographer.

Nicole loves travel and all things electronic, and she considers herself a bit of a "foodie." She started UrbanBytes photography as a creative outlet and as a way to still the moments and motions of everyday life.

She currently resides in Atlanta, Georgia, with her partner, Tiffany, and their two dogs, Lenny and Domino.

SLEEPING WITH THE ENEMY

Denise Writer

It's been fifteen years since Paige died, since her life was taken from her because her husband cheated on her with another man and gave her HIV. Now, I am not upset that he was gay, but I hate that his decision to live on the "down low" cost my friend her life.

I am still angry about it, angry that Paige married her husband when it was evident to everyone that he was gay; angry that her husband wasn't strong enough to walk away from the marriage instead of cheating on her with other men; angry with God for letting such a beautiful person suffer and then die the way she did. Time has not healed the wound of losing her from my life because I am still angry.

The Strength of My Soul

As I sit here with tears in my eyes watching the video she left in which she speaks to those who mattered most in her life, I am saddened. But I am also encouraged because, in this video, she says, "Write your book!" So, to honor her, one of the best friends I've ever had, I am writing.

It was our first day at a new job, and for some odd reason, Paige and I just gravitated to each other. She was pretty; she had a bright smile that lit up a room and such an infectious laugh. For our first week at my new job, she and I were inseparable. We exchanged numbers and talked at night like old friends. I can't remember connecting with anyone so quickly, especially since I'd never really had a lot of girlfriends in my life. She had such a positive spirit that it made you want to have her around.

During our second week of work, I felt very ill. Paige urged me to see my doctor because I did not look well. The next day, I visited the doctor and was asked if I might be pregnant. My husband and I had planned to start a family soon, but not at that moment. I took a pregnancy test, and it was positive. I was floored. I took a blood test to confirm, and yes, I was pregnant.

When I got to work, I told Paige, and she was

elated! But I was afraid to say anything to anyone else because I'd just started my job. When I got home that night, I told my husband that we were pregnant, and he was beyond excited. He picked me up and swung me around. We both laughed and cried at the excitement. Later that night, I went to take a shower and saw that I was bleeding. I gasped at the sight and called for my husband. He looked at me with terror in his eyes, and with the doctor's urging, we immediately went to the ER.

I called Paige, who said she was coming to the hospital. Not too long after we arrived, Paige showed up. I was so appreciative of her moral support and thought, "This is a true friend." After running some tests to make sure I was not having a miscarriage, they sent me home and ordered me to remain in bed until the doctor released me. I remained in bed for two weeks, and every day Paige came to see me. I began to think, this is the kind of woman I would like to be the godmother of my child. She was there for me every time I needed her. Even my husband liked her. He often said we looked alike and called her my sister.

After a few weeks, I was released from bed rest and returned to work. Paige and I were having lunch one day when I asked her to be the godmother of my child. She smiled from ear to ear and told me she would be delighted. That day, our friendship-sisterhood bond grew even stronger.

During the remainder of my pregnancy, we spent time together, shopping for baby clothes and furniture, doing as much as we could together. She said she wanted to be at the hospital when I went into labor, but my husband thought that was crossing the line, so he waited until I gave birth to our daughter to call Paige. She was there the next morning with gifts in hand for her new goddaughter. Paige was truly the most wonderful friend a person could have. She took her new goddaughter to get her ears pierced because I was too afraid to. She took my daughter for the weekends so my husband and I could have some time alone. Spending time with my daughter made Paige want children of her own.

At the time, she was dating a professional football player, a relationship she thought would lead to marriage, until he began to beat on her. Whenever his team would lose a game, he would hit her. Whenever she would find out he was cheating, he would hit her. It took over a year for her to get out of that relationship and away from him. After that, she had a string of bad luck with men, one after the other. Paige felt hopeless. Even spending time with her goddaughter and me didn't seem to bring her the same joy she once had because she, too, wanted to be married and to have children.

A few months passed, and out of the blue Paige told me that she had met someone. I was shocked and surprised but happy for her. She was a good catch, and I was hoping that this time, the man she was dating would appreciate her. She made him out to be Prince Charming. She would tell me how he doted on her, would shower her with gifts, and spend lots of time with her. He had already taken her to meet his family. He would even go with her when she got her hair done. I thought that was odd. What man wants to sit in a beauty salon with cackling women for hours? I was concerned, because they seemed to be moving so fast, but I kept my concerns to myself.

Paige said that a man had never treated her so well, and that she was falling in love with him. I voiced my concerns to my husband, who encouraged me to speak with Paige about what I was feeling, but again, I said nothing. I didn't want to put a damper on her happiness; she

The Strength of My Soul

deserved it. Plus, Paige wanted me to meet him, and I looked forward to giving him the third degree to make sure he was a good match for her. She told me that he was coming to have lunch with her one afternoon at work, and I could meet him then.

As I pulled into the parking lot returning from my lunch break, I saw a man walk out of the parking lot. He was dressed very neatly, hair cut very nicely; he was a sharp-looking man. He ran across the street to move out of the way of my vehicle, and my first thought was that he was gay. I didn't know him, but the way he moved, which was very effeminate, caught my attention. I went on my way and parked my car, returning to work. When I got to my office, Paige walked in and had the young man I had seen in the parking lot with her. She introduced him as her boyfriend, Darren. I was speechless. I didn't respond for what seemed like an eternity. He held out his hand to shake my hand, and I kind of stumbled through my words, eventually telling him it was nice to meet him.

Paige said they were heading out to lunch, and that she would talk with me later. I sat in silence wondering why she had chosen to date this man when he was so obviously gay. I began to think, maybe he's not gay and I'm overreacting. Maybe he was gay and had been delivered from homosexuality. Maybe Paige has been through so much horror with men that she no longer cared and would be with anyone who treated her well. I was at a complete loss.

When I got home that night, Paige called me to talk about Darren. I was silent. I told her I didn't know what to say, but that as long as she was happy, I was happy for her. My husband and I were planning to have a dinner party that weekend, so I invited Paige and her new beau. We had a great time. Darren fit in with our crowd. He talked, laughed, and joked like he had always been a friend with our friends. Paige and Darren had to leave early, and as soon as they left, everyone asked me if he was gay. At that moment, I knew I had to say something to Paige, because if others thought what I thought, then I probably wasn't wrong.

A few days later, I asked Paige to meet me for drinks after work and she obliged. We did some catching up, and I told her what was going on with her goddaughter. She then filled me in on what was going on in her life with Darren. I told her I had some concerns about him and wanted to discuss them with her. She told me she already knew what I was going to say, and that she had the same concerns in the beginning. She had originally thought he was gay, too. She said he assured her that he was not. She also said that when she met him, he had a gay roommate and she thought it odd for a straight man to be living with such an openly gay man. She shared that Darren's roommate even attacked him one night when he found out Paige was there, but he again assured her that he was not gay.

By now my mouth was hanging open in shock. I couldn't understand why she would date a man that *she'd* even thought was gay when she met him. She continued by letting me know that she was tired of dealing with men who treated her badly, and that Darren was the first man to ever be so kind and loving. I backed off and let her enjoy her relationship.

A few months later, they were engaged, and I was named a bridesmaid. I wanted so badly to tell Paige to run and never look back, because I knew that she was making a huge mistake. But I kept silent. I kept telling myself if she could accept Darren, then who am I to judge? But I did judge. I loved her, and it was hurting me to see her make a mistake that I knew some day she would regret. I always believed Darren would leave her for another man. I never in my wildest dreams imagined what the future had in store for them.

Almost a year later, they were married in a small ceremony of about seventy-five people. It was a beautiful wedding. The flowers were gorgeous, all of the décor was impeccable, and Paige was a breathtaking bride. She and Darren seemed very happy, and I tried to be happy for them. After the wedding, we would occasionally do couples things together, Paige, Darren, my husband and me. Now that Paige was married and Darren was so "attentive," all of our girlfriend outings became nonexistent because Darren went everywhere with her. I have to admit that I was jealous and missed my friend.

Within the year, Paige was pregnant, and the following year she and Darren gave birth to a beautiful baby boy. Paige was overjoyed, but it seemed her marriage started to take a turn for the worse. Darren became distant, and they began to have problems with intimacy. He traveled for work and seemed to be gone a lot more than usual. Paige complained to me that their sex life had diminished. She thought Darren wasn't attracted to her anymore. She said she would touch him, and his body was completely unresponsive. She had no idea what was happening. I tried to console her and show as much support as I could, but deep down, I knew what the problem was.

Darren became ill and had to be hospitalized. He had pneumonia. I prayed for Paige and her family and let her know that I was there for whatever they needed. His recovery was long and slow, but eventually he was back on his feet. One weekend, Paige and I attended a friend's baby shower, and she told me that she'd found a lump in her breast. I wasn't concerned because I'd found several in mine a few years prior and it turned out to be nothing. We were so young then that I didn't think there was cause for concern. I tried to reassure her, but I could see the fear in her eyes. She scheduled a doctor's appointment, and once seen they scheduled her for a biopsy. A few weeks later, she told me that everything was fine. I knew it would be. We went on with life as normal.

While away on family vacation, I received a call from Paige. She said it was urgent that she speak with me. That worried me, but I was all ears. She reminded me of the biopsy that she'd had months prior and informed me that she lied about her results. She told me that she had lymphoma, which was caused by the HIV virus. Immediately, I burst into tears and had to pull over on the side of the highway. I was enraged because I knew that her positive HIV status was Darren's fault. I started to scream and cry hysterically. She also told me they found out that he was HIV positive when he had pneumonia the year before. She got tested immediately and discovered that she had been infected as well. She didn't tell me at the time because she felt I would treat her differently, because HIV was still very new and we did not have all of the facts about how to contract it and its effects on the body.

Paige's diagnosis ripped my heart apart. Paige informed me that she was starting chemotherapy right away because her lymphoma was very aggressive and causing her a great deal of bone pain. As soon as I got back into town from my vacation, I went to see her, and I continued to see her weekly. She began to lose her hair, but she was a trooper and never let it bother her. Paige said lymphoma gave her an opportunity to experiment with wigs. Although Darren wasn't intimately attracted to Paige anymore, he was always there by her side, being supportive.

The Strength of My Soul

As time passed, the chemo seemed to be working, and after about eleven months, Paige's cancer was in remission, or so we thought. After being off chemo for a month, Paige woke up in excruciating pain one night and could barely move. Darren rushed her to the hospital, and after extensive testing, it was determined her cancer had come back and was more aggressive. This time it was in her bones. She was scheduled for radiation and shortly after began chemo again. After receiving treatments for almost another year, it appeared that her cancer had gone into remission. She was always so upbeat and joking. It seemed as if what was happening to her didn't bother her, but I knew deep down she had to be scared. I was terrified. I was moving out of the state for work, and I hated leaving her with everything that was going on. One night, I got on my knees and begged God to let her be okay and to fully recover from this. I pleaded and cried to God. My cries went unanswered.

Before I moved, I spent time with Paige. While sitting and chatting in her living room, her husband walked into the room holding a dress. I looked at him strangely, and Paige said, "I want you to have this." I looked at her, and she smiled. I asked her why she wanted me to have the dress, and she told me she just wanted me to have it. Deep down I knew that she was trying to give me a part of her to hold on to. Her husband also handed me a VHS tape, and when I asked what it was, she said she recorded messages to the people closest to her. My heart sank because I felt like she was saying goodbye to me, and I wasn't ready.

I moved that following week. It was hard, but I had to go. Paige and I talked every other day, and she kept me up to date on her treatment. After being gone for seven months and assuming everything was well because Paige led me to believe all was well, I received a call from Darren letting me know that things were not okay. He informed me that I needed to come see Paige as soon as I could. I asked him what he considered soon, and he said, "this week."

I immediately called my boss and said that I needed to leave because my sister was ill and needed me. That night, I got on the road, and the next morning I was at Paige's house by her side. What I saw left me speechless.

Her cancer had spread so severely that it had disfigured her body. She was swollen, and the side of her body where the cancer had started was completely open. I tried to keep a brave face, but I was truly horrified. She was suffering, and I wanted to kill the culprit, her husband, who was walking around pain-free and normal. Paige and I sat for hours and talked. She told me she had forgiven Darren and had made peace with her life. She knew that she was going to die, and she was okay with it. The only thing that bothered her was not being able to be there to watch her son grow up.

I spent that week with Paige. I got there on a Tuesday. She passed away that Saturday morning. That was fifteen years ago. My heart still aches. I was angry and bitter for a long time. I stopped praying. I stopped going to church. I was mad at God for allowing this to happen. Where was his grace and mercy? Why did he let her suffer so horribly? Paige did not deserve any of this. For the first couple of weeks after her death, I cried daily because I would pick up the phone to call her and realize I couldn't. I would never hear her voice again. It broke me.

One night, several weeks after her death, Paige came to me in a dream. She came through the front door of my house, walked over to me, and put her hand on my face. She called my name and said, "I am okay." She smiled, turned around, and walked away. I immediately woke up crying.

After I calmed down, I thought, "She said she is okay. She is okay, so I have to be okay." I prayed that night for peace. Although the pain didn't go away, I did feel better.

A few years later, Darren developed lymphoma and died shortly after.

Today, I am better. I still miss her, but I am better. She taught me true forgiveness and showed me what true love is, and I try to honor that in every part of my life. It is so hard to lose people who have had such an impact on your life, but I remind myself that although they are not with us in the physical form, they are always with us in our memories, in our dreams and in our hearts. They will always love us.

I love and miss you, Paige, and I am writing this for you.

Denise Writer has always had a desire to be a writer. At the age of four, she wrote short stories and plays that she and her sister used to perform for her family and friends. As Denise got older, her desire grew stronger to be a part of the literary world.

This year, Denise is finally tackling her first book project by participating in this anthology.

Stories From My Womb

STATISTICALLY SPEAKING

Angelia Henderson

Eleanor Roosevelt once said, "We gain strength, and courage, and confidence by each experience in which we really stop to look fear in the face. We must do that which we think we cannot." If that's the gospel truth, it explains why I was able to make it through, because if it weren't for that way of thinking, I honestly don't know where I would be or how my life would have turned out. In all honesty, I was staring fear squarely in the face and my faith was taking a severe beating. At the tender age of thirteen, life reared its unpredictable head and announced that fun and games were over. As I reflect on my life now, I am amazed that a child could successfully navigate the hardships that for most adults would be daunting. Statistically speaking, I survived and succeeded against all odds. I realize that I am more than a conqueror!

I was born in small-town America where everyone knew everyone, and everyone knew each other's business. For some, a social life was attending church; for others, it involved drinking, smoking, and having sex. Even though teen sex was very much a part of the social fabric of the town, discussion of sexuality was considered taboo. It was never openly discussed. Instead, it was whispered among the elders and not shared with the most impressionable members of the community. No one took the time to explain the changes happening to our young bodies, how to handle menstrual cycles, what biological changes occurred in boys and girls, and what happened when the two worlds collided.

I was reared by my paternal grandmother, who was somewhat old-fashioned in her approach to menstrual cycles, sex, and pregnancy. Her advice to me was, "Keep your dress down and your panties up." That was it. She didn't elaborate, and I had no idea what she meant; I just knew not to ask. Back then, it seemed that children didn't have those types of conversations with their parents. What I did know was that a number of my friends and acquaintances were doing "it" long before I knew what "it" was.

It's sad to say that my maiden voyage into sex resulted in me getting pregnant.

My life was drastically changed on July 2, 1975, at the county hospital. I vividly remember how incredibly cold, white, sterile, and bright the room was. There was the occasional sound of metal rebounding off metal, muted voices giving instructions, and the constant beeping sounds of machines. I attempted to wrap my thirteen-year-old mind around what was happening to me. I was only thirteen, not much living at that point. Other numbers started to crowd my brain. I had been in pain for almost nine hours, and I was nine months pregnant. You read that right, I was about to become a mother at the ripe old age of thirteen after becoming pregnant at the age of twelve. I had not planned to be a mother, and the fifteen-year-old father had not planned to be a dad. We had done the one thing that should have been reserved for responsible adults – have sex. As I lay in the cold hospital room, I realized that there was no turning back, no do-overs. I didn't know what to expect or how my life would be changed.

The nursing attendant was as gentle and reassuring as she could be. "Take deep breaths, baby," she instructed. "They'll give you something a little later to ease the pain." The pain was excruciating – my back felt as though it was being used as a punching bag by a heavyweight boxer. I wailed and moaned each time a contraction wracked my body. The pain in my back was relentless and seemed to be intensifying. My genital area was equally besieged by intense, excruciating pain. I had neither been forewarned nor prepared for what awaited me with childbirth. Why would anyone feel the need to explain to a teenager the anxiety and pain associated with bringing a child into the world? As far as they were concerned, I should have still been playing with Barbie dolls, experimenting with make-up, or playing kickball or dodgeball with the other neighborhood children. I should not be in a hospital about to give birth.

Eventually, I was wheeled into a private hospital room to await the attending physician's arrival. At that point, I had been in labor for twelve hours and still had no idea what was about to happen in my life. I had only received prenatal care twice at the local health clinic. By the time I had my first visit, I was already five months pregnant. I was always somewhat husky, and the pregnancy was hidden from plain view, though not intentionally. The change in my physical appearance had gone unnoticed, even by those closest to me. Since I played sports, my menstrual cycle was sporadic. When I started to miss my cycle, I did not equate it to me being pregnant. Again, the correlation between sex and pregnancy had not entered my young mind. I never experienced morning sickness. Only when my abdomen started to swell did I realize that "something" was wrong.

The nurse came in and measured how far I had dilated. To my dismay, I had barely made a blip on the dilation radar. It seemed my son had his own idea of when he wanted to make my acquaintance; he was taking his own sweet time. At that point, it was determined that an epidural was needed. I didn't know what an epidural was; however, the nurse stated that it would substantially ease my pain. That was the first great news I had received since I was raced to the hospital at 10:00 p.m. the previous day.

The nurse returned a few minutes later with a needle filled with medication that I hoped would give me some relief. She injected the needle's contents into my IV bag, and I felt instantly warm. She then had me turn on my side. She swabbed my lower back, had me remain absolutely still, and injected me in my lower back. Though initially uncomfortable, the results were well worth it. I no longer felt the excruciating back pain I had endured hours earlier. Finally, I was allowed to lie on my back and I drifted into an exhausted slumber. I'm not sure how long I slept – I was suddenly awakened by an audible "pop" and the warm the sensation of liquid flooding my hospital bed. I pressed the call button, and the nurses immediately appeared. They indicated that my water had broken and it was time for me to be moved to the delivery room.

I was again whisked away to another cold, brightly lit room filled with faces covered with masks and concern. "She's just a baby," I remember someone exclaiming. They went about prepping me for the birth of my child, covering my shivering, young body with sheets and placing my feet in stirrups. After being taken to the delivery room, my recollection of the events is somewhat hazy. I just remember it taking – or so I thought – less than twenty minutes to push. By the time my son was born, I had endured eighteen hours of labor.

Angelia Henderson

Some twelve hours later, a nurse brought my son into my room and placed him in my arms. I remember how good he smelled and how tiny he was. His head was covered in straight, black hair, and his face was round and angelic. I set about checking his fingers, toes, and ears – heck, his whole little body. He was absolutely perfect. The nurse returned with a bottle and instructed me on how to feed him. She asked if I would breastfeed him. Honestly, I had no idea what that entailed, so I said no. Two days after giving birth, I was released from the hospital. Once home, the flood of support and visitors were overwhelming but needed. I was petrified and unsure of my future. Would I finish school? Would I get pregnant again? Would my friends and family abandon me?

Home was with my grandmother, who was the mother of ten children. She had become my surrogate mother when I was seven years old when my biological mother (who was also a teen mother) was murdered. After the birth of my son, she was matter-of-fact that I was no longer a child. I was now someone's mother, and it was up to me to care for him. My days started early every morning with feedings, changing diapers, soothing his cries when he didn't feel well – everything expected of a new parent, albeit a much older one. I had to deal with doctor's visits, teething, potty training, chicken pox, finding suitable babysitters, and a host of other day-to-day parenting issues. Many times I was angry and despondent that I had gotten myself in this situation. I could no longer come and go as I pleased. Once, I missed my high school seniors honor program because my son had chickenpox. There were times when I was unable to play in volleyball games because I could not find a babysitter. I had to put away childish things and behaviors in order to become a responsible adult.

All of my family members are high achievers, and the thought that I would not rise to meet the educational bar they had set was unimaginable. I had always wanted to attend college and become a writer. However, with the birth of my son, I knew that would be a major undertaking. I would rise early to feed, bathe, and deliver my son to the babysitter's house before walking to school each morning. Once I left school at 3:00, I picked him up from the sitter's, headed home to repeat the morning's routine, and do homework. Mind you, I was fourteen at the time. I felt overwhelmed and wanted to give up. I knew I couldn't let my son, my grandmother, or myself down. I wanted her to be proud of me and to repay her for being my rock and staunchest supporter. Thus, I set about studying harder and being more focused in order to graduate.

Thankfully, his father stepped in and provided as much support as he could. From day one, it was never a question of if he would be present; it was always what he could do to help me achieve my dream of getting through school and eventually attending college. However, he was also a teen trying to navigate the role of parenthood. We experienced hiccups, missteps, and blunders along the way. But with the help of family, friends, and strangers, we were able to rear a healthy, happy son. We both returned to school and graduated. I did everything that most sixteen, seventeen, and eighteen year olds did – sports, school clubs, becoming co-vice president of the senior class. I even attended proms.

While my experience may read like a made-for-television movie, that was not the case. I give all thanks and honor to God for blessing me with a solid family foundation. My grandmother was instrumental in how I reared my son. She never made me feel ashamed of the fact that I was so young when I gave birth to him. I am grateful because it would have been easy enough to go the way of many teen mothers: having more babies, dropping out of school, and becoming a statistic. Instead, she encouraged me to succeed at all cost and to dismiss the naysayers. I remember one teacher lecturing me about my pregnancy. She did not want me to participate in the local spelling bee due to my "condition." She didn't feel that I was a good representative of the school, even though I was an excellent speller. Needless to say, that was just one of the hurdles I was able to clear.

Thanks to the support and the unconditional love I received from the community, I graduated with honors, received a few scholarships, and graduated from Georgia State University in 1985, 2,921.94 days after giving birth to my son. After graduating with a Bachelors of Arts degree in Journalism, I started a career in the legal field, which has spanned almost twenty-five years.

Current statistics regarding teen pregnancies in my home state are alarming: according to the Alabama Campaign to Prevent Teen Pregnancy, "Alabama has one of the highest teen childbearing rates in the United States. In 2008, there was an estimated 12,257 teen pregnancies in our state; a rate of 39.2 (females age 10-19). Of these pregnancies, 8,567 resulted in live births." My intent is not to paint a rosy picture regarding teen pregnancy; reality and honesty make more sense. Had I known the hardships, uncertainty, and stigma associated with being an unwed, teen mother, I would not have traveled the uncharted territory of having sex. Did my son's father and I have any idea how a moment's indiscretion would affect our futures? My answer is a resounding NO! We were just two children, whose curiosity got the better of them, and it changed the trajectory of our respective lives.

I beat the odds, and I want to advise other teenagers contemplating becoming sexually active: *don't*! If you're dead set on buckling under peer pressure and not listening to your parents, be ready to live with the consequences. Though my son was unplanned, he was never unwanted. You've got to realize that repeating the same behavior of having unprotected sex can and will land you in the same predicament – unplanned pregnancies, or worse, sexually transmitted diseases. It won't be a skate in the park being a teen parent.

Having a pregnant teenager is never a parent's

hope or dream. Parents want their children to grow up happy and carefree. So to the parents: be there unconditionally for your children and have open and honest discussions regarding your child's biological changes and sexual risk-taking behavior. Although there are no guarantees that the plans parents make for their children will come to fruition, being there for your child through unplanned circumstances and situations, one of them being pregnancy, will help your child become a positive and productive member of society. My desire to achieve a certain level of greatness was born out of watching my grandmother work in a cotton mill for over thirty years, sell Avon products, and be a hairdresser just to provide for her family. She always had a measure of stick-to-itiveness regarding hard work. That is truly a reflection of my work ethic today.

I've been perceived as an exception to the statistical rule regarding teen pregnancies and the success rate of reaching adulthood without succumbing to society's pressures. When I became pregnant, my family did not disown me or abandon me. That's not to say that there weren't occasions when we did not see eye-to-eye on my parenting skills. I know that God places many people in our lives in different seasons for different reasons, but the paradigm remains the same: the type of energy you put out will be returned to you tenfold. Your thoughts must be of positivity, empowerment, enlightenment, success, and dedication. Those are the thoughts that evoke a can-do posture, proving that your self-worth and your ability to rise above your current station in life is attainable.

Angelia R. Henderson originally hails from Roanoke, Alabama. After graduating from Handley High School in 1981, she set her sights on furthering her education at Georgia State University. In 1985, Angelia received a Bachelors of Arts Degree in Journalism. Since then, she's worn many career hats for well-known companies like Smith, Gambrell & Russell, LLP; Swift Currie McGhee & Hiers, LLP; and KMPG, LLP. Today, she works as a legal assistant for The Weather Channel, LLP. In her spare time, Angelia enjoys writing poetry and short stories, reading, photography, traveling, volunteering, and spending time with her family and friends. Her son, Julian, recently celebrated his fortieth birthday. Angelia subscribes to the notion that equanimity and her faithful journey with God have enabled her to persevere no matter the obstacles.

Hebrew 11:1 *"Now FAITH is being sure of what we hope for and certain of what we do not see."*

KEEP SHOWING UP FOR LOVE

Dr. Vikki Johnson

I am not my Sister's Keeper, but I am my Sister! Every time I say those words, they touch me to my core. It seems my entire life has been about becoming acquainted with the myriad of emotions women feel. I feel like I'm best friends with LOVE itself, which is a beautiful thing. As far back as I can remember, I have been what some call a "hopeless romantic." I love me some LOVE. I love to watch people in love. I enjoy love songs. I get excited when people I love find love. And of course, sometimes my love of love has gotten me into situations that taught me some painful lessons about love.

I have been betrayed by people who said they loved me, and I have been blessed by people who said they love me. Love has transformed me, but it took me consistently showing up again and again, willing to "make love" all the time in every situation, even the ugly ones that made me feel less than whole. I didn't always think this way. I have had some amazing relationships that have made me who I am today. I am sure you, too, have had some wonderful relationships (at least they started that way) that have taught you much.

Love has walked me through divorce, miscarriage, abortions, and post-partum depression. It has also led me to the most beautiful relationship of my adult life, the one with my daughter. When I wanted to give up, my daughter kept me going. She is a precious gift from God, and I thank God daily for entrusting me with pouring into her. At the same time, I can't help but think how different my life would be if the other three – yes, three – I conceived had been born and a part of my world. I still get sad at times, even as I write this, to imagine "what could have been" if today I was responsible for three daughters and one son.

My first pregnancy ended in a miscarriage. I remember that period in my life like it was yesterday. I was a junior in college, on a full athletic scholarship, and a member of the gospel choir, and my sorority was in the midst of pledging a line. I was excited about being pregnant. I was so excited that I was fearless and ready to defend my decision to have a baby in spite of what it would cost me. I was willing to walk away from my basketball scholarship and from people's opinions, even the people who were the most disappointed in me. The baby's father wanted me to have an abortion, but I adamantly refused, telling him that he could leave and never come back. The baby and I would be fine, even if I had to do it alone. I remember the night I went into premature labor at twelve weeks. It was 1986. I was in the emergency room alone, afraid, and very angry that I had just lost a baby girl that I wanted so badly. Right then and there, I made a conscious, sincere commitment to the Lord.

In the midst of trauma, my relationship with God truly began. That night, God let me know that He was with me, even though the baby's father wasn't. Years later, after the birth of my daughter, I got pregnant from someone whom I loved and still deeply love, but the relationship was a secret. It's ironic how "before accepting Christ" I was fearless, courageous, and willing to go through fire to have my baby. But this time it was different. I was scared, alone, fearful, and bound by thoughts of shame, humiliation, rejection, intimidation, abandonment, and other people's opinions. What would the church think? What would I tell my pastor and his wife? What would my family think about the "golden child"? The baby's father was caught in the same web of questions. He persuaded me that we both had "too much to lose" if I had the baby, so I had an abortion. I aborted our son, another baby I badly wanted. The baby's father paid for the abortion, and that was the extent of his involvement. As far as I'm concerned, I went through that experience alone, too. Once again, God let me know that He was with me, even if the baby's father wasn't.

At first, I felt relief. Then the thoughts of regret, anger, resentment, hurt, and loss began to periodically overwhelm me. What had I done? Why did I do it? I had an abortion so EVERYBODY ELSE would be okay. But what about me? There I was, "in Christ," where I should have been the most secure, feeling insecure and fragile. I wondered if this was something I would have to deal with for the rest of my life.

A few years later, I was doing okay until I got pregnant AGAIN in yet another "secret relationship." This time, I thought about what I wanted and how happy this baby would make me. However, that did not last long. The baby's father and I were both married to other people. Too many people would be hurt. Too many lives would be affected and thrust into turmoil. I thought about taking my daughter, running away, and having the baby on my own. Desperate people do desperate things, right? Who was I kidding. I could not do that either. So, after much thought and discussion with the baby's father, I convinced myself AGAIN that aborting our unborn daughter was the best thing for everybody else. This time, the relief lasted only a few hours. Later that same day, the waves of guilt and regret began to wash over me, and with that same intensity, lasted for the next several months. I remember attending my grandmother's funeral during this time and completely breaking down in tears as soon as I saw her in the casket. Yes, I was sad that she was gone, but for the first time, I felt the anguish of conceiving but not having three babies.

After that, I would cry only if no one was around. I hid my pain from people. Once again, God let me know that He was there, because I was holding so much inside I should have exploded. Eventually, I cried out to God, telling Him how sorry I was for rejecting His gifts. I also told God that I needed help because I could not live like that anymore. The guilt was secretly taking over my life. The first thing God did was "turn up" His love for me through my daughter. She was and still is my "earth angel." The next thing God did was allow me to hear a Christian radio broadcast one morning while driving to work. I was on the interstate listening to Pastor Jack Hayford minister to women who had had abortions. I was stunned, but his words were very soothing. He then encouraged his listeners to request his book, *I'll Hold You In Heaven*.

That book was the beginning of my healing. The reassurance that I will see my children again provoked me to go after God with all that's within me. Each time I conceived, my children became a part of me forever. I still have sentimental moments every now and then. The difference in my life now is that I fully embrace and engage the love of God, and the security found in that love. His love made provisions for my mistakes and bad choices. His love nurtures my children in heaven until I get there to be reunited with them. His love forgives me and enables me to forgive myself.

I can't stop the moments of regret from coming, but I don't invite them to stay around either. The last thing I did (and maybe this will help someone) was to create a memorial for the children I had conceived and never made it. The memorial itself is not as important as the fact that you made the memorial. You can plant a garden, add charms to your bracelet or necklace in your child's memory, or start a project or business. Whatever you do, don't act like it never happened, because it did. Honor your child's memory in a way that's meaningful to you. There are many options. The beauty is that this time, you can choose something that brings life back to your life. Now when I show up for love, I bring love with me and the results have been just lovely! Sis, keep showing up for love!

Dr. Vikki Johnson, CDKA, is a sought-after speaker, author, mentor, chaplain, sisterhood advocate, living kidney donor, and a proud Mom. She is a graduate of Howard University with a Bachelors of Arts in Broadcast Management. She also received degrees from the Calvary Bible Institute and the CICA University & Seminary, with an Honorary Doctorate of Divinity, Chaplaincy and Ambassador-at-Large designation.

A thought-provoking speaker, Dr. Vikki has influenced thousands of women over the last twenty years and has been featured as a keynote speaker for TEDx Women, the Pentagon, the Department of Commerce, as well as various women's conferences, retreats, and workshops.

She is also the CEO of Authentic Living Enterprises, which includes her signature media brand, GIRL TALK UNPLUGGED, and the creator of SOUL WEALTH ACADEMY, a mentoring experience for women. Dr. Vikki says that as a result of working with my company, women break up with the status quo in their life. They no longer live in survival mode, but live a life of undeniable purpose. Unstuck, they move through the world with clarity, confidence, and self- worth.

A bestselling author, she has touched thousands with her pen and has written eight books. Dr. Vikki has been featured in Jet, Essence, Upscale, various blogs, and radio shows, and recently re-released her successful book, *Addicted To Counterfeit Love*. She has been the Associate Pastor of Women at Kingdom Worship Center in Towson, Maryland, since 1999. In addition, she received the 2014 Heritage and Community Service Award from the Friends of African American Research Library and Cultural Center in her hometown of Fort Lauderdale, Florida, for over fifteen years of community advocacy and empowerment.

Dr. Vikki Johnson

Dr. Vikki recently left BET Networks after eighteen years of dedicated service. There, she was responsible for the day-to-day efforts of the Emmy award-winning Rap-It-Up Campaign, the network's HIV/AIDS initiative, the network's partnership with Make-A-Wish Foundation, and other pro-social initiatives. Her career has spanned over thirty years in music, sports, entertainment, and community advocacy. In addition to her work, she is a proud member of Delta Sigma Theta Sorority, the National Association of Black Female Executives in Music and Entertainment (NABFEME), ColorComm (Women of Color In Communication), The BOSS (Bringing Out Successful Sisters) Network, and the National Association of Professional Women (NAPW).

Dr. Vikki also enjoys connecting with her audience through social media platforms. You can follow her on Twitter & Instagram @AllThingsVikki, connect with her on Facebook at Elder Vikki Johnson, or join her Girl Talk Unplugged A Sacred Sisterhood Community on Facebook and visit her website www.vikkijohnson.com

15

BRAVE NEW MULES

Mimi Gonzalez

"You're not a *real* woman. You've never given birth," said my favorite aunt. I knew I wasn't going to reproduce in this lifetime. "Technically, you *are* a biological failure," my mother offered in scientific consolation. She was right. I had not heeded the raison d'être of all life on this planet: to replicate one's DNA, making it stronger for the next generation. After all, adaptation and evolution require suitable vehicles to maintain the constant march of existence.

The only marching I did was in gay pride parades. Homosexuality, an act of expression in complete defiance of nature's call to mate. The adage "I wasn't born gay, my first boyfriend made me gay" was a punch line I had delivered for years to consistent laughter. "He rubbed me the wrong way," I would say.

My first sexual relationship was in college with an Islamic Middle Eastern man, an exchange student from Qatar. He tried to reassure my virginal self by recounting how he lost his. Two of his initial sexual explorations were tales of torture. His mother beat him when she caught him taking his turn among his friends on a Palestinian boy. A few years later, in his teens, his uncle took him to India to purchase the allaying of his sexuality through a prostitute, a tiny woman. "She kept saying 'pain, pain,' and I pretended to search my pockets for a pen," he laughed in the retelling. "I don't have a pen for you." No, he didn't. He had an enormous pencil full of lead that drew blood and left a tattoo I've never been able to erase.

The sexual frustration, the servitude, the near obedience he required from me because I was a woman was traumatic enough to inspire dreams of freedom dressed in gratification. After a typical five-minute romp after which he'd roll off into the slumber of satisfaction, I'd lay awake, my senses alerted but unanswered, fantasizing about watching pornography with him. Those coupled viewings were sometimes followed by a display of concern for my pleasure. Typically though, I dropped into the well of sleep and found comfort in my dreams. Two vivid, lucid dreams of sexual play with a woman friend of mine woke me in the night. And awoke something in me.

I knew how to please myself, so I knew it was possible. Sexual discovery led me to the vistas I knew were there, whereas his episodes left me stranded at the entrance to the park. I knew there were a beach and a deep sea of waves I could ride. There was even a cliff from which to jump or be taken to and pushed over by skilled lovers, where I could submerge into the dark waters of communion. Other women knew the way. They showed me. I took their hands. We brought each other into the dark feminine mystery.

But what of the mystery of mitosis? Life among Homo sapiens can't continue without the tiniest human cell of spermatozoa meeting the largest human cell of ovum and the two transforming in the dark earth of a womb. Been there, done that – inside my own mother, without whom I would not exist.

Motherhood, the first and finest act of construction, whose uterus builds, nurtures, and delivers bodies. I did not accomplish that with my body. I did not actualize its full female potential. I chose to be like a mule, a sterile animal that cannot reproduce but is strong and independent – maybe because she knows she's the end of the line. She knows the purpose of her life is not reproduction—nature's whole scheme of things—so she has to define her life for her own damn self since she'll never be a dam.

I didn't realize I was a mule until menopause, as I rode the last few years of my female cycle into the sunset alone. My mother warned, "There's a world of misery for a life of hedonism. If you don't have children, you'll be empty." When I held a friend's infant or watched kids at a playground discover and delight in the world, I would wonder if she were right. I tightrope- walked carefully over the breeding abyss and declared, "I don't regret not having children, I lament it." Words came to save and define me. After counseling at an LGBT youth camp I attended with other teenagers for a week, my conviction was confirmed. Teenagers are so rude and dismissive they'll convince anyone who hasn't bred it's an acceptable choice.

Is a woman who chooses not to reproduce a threat to the species, or its salvation? I declare that choice to be exclusively female, at once a deeply revolutionary and evolutionary act. Choosing infertility defies physical laws. It is bringing consciousness to the natural order of flesh. By doing so, a mule woman stands as a living testament to will, creating a visceral example for the teaming herd of humanity to witness. I am woman. I am barren. There is more.

I've met whole cities of mules during my big gay sojourn through life, each of us determined to show how well we can strut and draw suitors to our juicy, fully functioning and deliberately infertile grounds, all the while dancing Maypole reveries of fecundity to sterility. The great mating season was every weekend or night journey to a club where we'd do our best imitations of the mystery dance free of the consequence of pregnancy.

Mules may mate, but it is a barren enterprise. Does the jack mule care that his sperm creates nothing but satisfaction? Is the molly concerned that her void of creation lay bare? Maybe our sterilized pets bear their castrations in a depression that domesticates them or maybe they too revel in their individuation.

Only a female body can make this conscious evolutionary leap. Even if he chooses vasectomy, a man cannot make this choice. The male part of the reproduction equation is as small as punctuation – necessary, but not the descriptive part of the story. Every time a man's part of the formula leaves his body, he's done. He's played his role in reproduction with every orgasm. Every orgasm a woman has does nothing to transform the genetic storyline. Or does it?

The way stress can alter telomeres*, perhaps every female orgasm is changing female genetic coding all over the planet. One woman's sexual exploration breaks ground and reverberates to the women caged behind burkas or in heels, whispering something only their female form can hear: *"You do not have to use the deep space of your uterus for its purpose of reproducing. You can defy convention, alter nature, and become your own autonomous universe."*

There's the culturally subversive proposition we've been striving toward for millennia: self-determined women.

Barren women are great beasts of burden, packing the ideas of purpose and form into self- selected orgasms that produce something other than reproduction. Freed from the yoke of breeding, the sterile are ripe with ideas. We are the brave new mules leading the way to a pack of frightened

The Strength of My Soul

yet determined explorers navigating a harsh and demanding biological landscape. In the animal world, mules are strong, patient, and surefooted. They are highly intelligent creatures that eat less and are ready for the journey. Follow us, hop on our backs, and join the herd of human female mules. We're headed to a new promised land, and we'll surely find the way.

*Telomeres are caps at the end of each strand of DNA that protect chromosomes.

Ohio-born, Michigan-raised, Midwest Latina **Mimi Gonzalez** is a national touring comedian of twenty years who bears the soul of a poet named Noemi Rose. She writes because she breathes and publishes annually while maintaining her comedy career. She's been through the identity wars and still aims to reach the promised land of the one true race: humanity. She's honored to be included among the women in this book, whom she calls siStars. mimi@mimigonzalez.com

I AM A CHILDLESS MOTHER

Valerie Chanell Jones

It never occurred to me that there were some things I just wouldn't do. My destiny was to go to college, get married, and have a son. After all, I had a plan: finish college, marry by age twenty- four, and have the son that I had been having recurring dreams about by twenty-six. So, imagine my surprise when life derailed my well-laid plan. Now, looking back, I can see the ever-so- subtle signs that indicated my eventual fate: the t-shirt, given to me by a friend's mother, which depicted a woman crying and sitting alone with a caption that read, "I can't believe that I forgot to have children"; the reality that neither marriage nor pregnancy, even with calculated planning, didn't materialize. At twenty-six, I was seriously single. The relationship I had been in ended the same day that I received my masters degree. The love was there, but somehow the independence that attracted him, my desire for a career, and other things, didn't work for him. I was shocked, hurt, and angry, but I had to grin and bear it. After all, it was supposed to be a happy day, and too many friends and family had traveled to celebrate. I couldn't let them know how bad I felt inside, and chose to deal with my emotions on my own.

Upon entering the workforce, career development and advancement became my focus. I desired to be married before having children, and since marriage was taking a backseat in my life, the thought of pregnancy and motherhood also took a hit. To make matters worse, by twenty-seven it was discovered, through an annual doctor's visit, that I had four tiny fibroid tumors. Yes, the signs were there, but as is often the case, it is through hindsight that some of the most important events of life are truly made clear.

Since change is inevitable, the year 1992 began my years of reckoning, starting with the death of one of my closest friends. He was six years my senior, and his sickness and death stopped me in my tracks. I've always known that death is a part of life, but it wasn't supposed to happen then. He had too much to live for, and we had too much fun to have. And then he was gone. I had spent so many nights in the hospital with him that it felt odd to be alone.

Likewise, 1993 was even worse. In February of that year, my grandmother suddenly became ill, and by September, she was gone. My world, the world that worked for me, changed in an instant, and it hurt. I had never felt so much pain, pain so deep that no position I sat in, stood in, or lay in, brought me solace. I hurt to my soul. You see, I knew how to live *with* her, and now I was being forced to learn to live *without* her. Soul pain is the worst pain, and while I believe it can give birth to dreams, this felt more like a nightmare. It's strange, how the sickness or death of a loved one can force you to think of your own mortality and contribution to life.

During my next annual visit to my gynecologist, I started the conversation about pregnancy. Given the fibroid tumors, and the fact I had recently celebrated my thirty-second birthday, I was considered high-risk for first-time pregnancy. For this reason, I believed it to be a good time for us to talk. Options and risks were discussed, and I left his office with information and a decision to make. Realizing that my biological clock was now banging as loudly as the Liberty Bell, it didn't take long to decide that it was now or never.

Two years passed, and I was still not pregnant. I knew there had to be a problem, and it wasn't that I wasn't trying. I scheduled a doctor's visit that turned into several doctor's visits. I can't remember how many different types of ultrasounds came later, but they all revealed the same thing: those tiny fibroid tumors had grown quickly, and they were taking over. They had grown so quickly that it was possible the fibroids were not my only issue. There was no way to know, though, except through surgery. With this revelation came more information to read and consider so I could make a decision for myself and for any child that I may have.

My doctor discussed options, myomectomy versus hysterectomy, and was hopeful that we would be dealing with only fibroid tumors. Knowing that I wanted a child, my doctor was a proponent for the myomectomy. The process would include shrinking the fibroids first, then surgically removing as many as possible to hopefully preserve the uterus for pregnancy. I asked about the probability of a successful pregnancy after going through the pre-surgical process, the actual surgery, and everything associated after surgery in preparation for "possible" pregnancy, and was told I had a fifty percent chance of success. My heart dropped. He might as well have said I had a zero percent change, because to me, that's what fifteen percent equated to.

I was ready to be a mother, but to go through this process and come home without a baby was not acceptable. That kind of disappointment would be too hard to bear. So that day, after calming my inner shock and protesting to God, I made the decision to have a hysterectomy instead of a myomectomy. I decided my own parental fate because I didn't trust that I could handle the negative odds. Eighteen days after my thirty-fifth birthday, the surgery was completed with no complications and nothing more than my uterus removed. I was very happy to be awakened to the voice of my doctor saying, "You did well, the right choice was made, and there is no cancer." I would later learn that my uterus was comparable to the size of a woman five months pregnant, and full of nothing but fibroid tumors. I've heard that as long as there is breath there is hope. That day represents the most painful of all miscarriages, because my legacy died. There would never be a child born to me – all breath was gone. I felt grateful and empty at the same time. Upon my release, I recuperated in my mother's home and enjoyed Thanksgiving, Christmas, and New Year's Day as I convalesced. I never experienced indigestion or pain of any type thanks to a great doctor and an even greater God!

Life after surgery, for the most part, seemed normal; but I have to admit that acceptance has its peaks and valleys. Sometimes I was caught off guard with people's bold comments. I should say that I don't believe everyone said these things actually meant harm, but the words hurt. They would say things like, "Why did you allow him to take away your womanhood?" Or they'd say, "You're just half of a woman now." Church provided no safety net either. I remember vividly after a Mother's Day Sunday Service, not long after the surgery, when a young boy ran to me with a rose in hand saying, "Happy Mother's Day, Miss Valerie!" He proudly presented his rose, hugged me, and ran back into the sanctuary of the church. Just as I turned to leave, one of the "seasoned" mothers of the church said, "You need to give that rose back, you ain't no mother." I looked in her eyes and walked away. I chose to walk away and not tell her what I thought of her and her comment. To me, it was better to give her the respect that she refused to give to me.

That walk, though, was one of the longest of my life, and by the time I reached my car, I was choking back tears. At the same time, others started asking questions about adoption. Some would ask me whether I would adopt, and others would ask me when I would do it. I hadn't kept my surgery a secret, but I hated being asked those questions. After all, I was still struggling with the fact that I would never bear a child, questioning why I couldn't have children when so many women have them and don't want them. I was looking for justification, the blessing.

Soon, I started to consider adoption. Truthfully, it is a wonderful process, and it fills a desire and need for those on both sides. Children are placed in families that provide the love and safety that the natural parents could not provide, and adoptive parents have their parenting desires fulfilled. But the more adoption became an option, the more I knew that it wasn't the process to "motherhood" for me. This knowledge added to my woes. I felt awful for not wanting to adopt, because I knew there were and still are many children that need love. The emptiness of not knowing my own, though, kept me frozen.

"Unsolicited adoption" opinions, coupled with my inward pressure about surgery and adoption decisions, took me to a darker place than I had ever experienced before. I knew that my countenance was different, but I didn't recognize that I was depressed until I wasn't anymore. God is good, and He is merciful.

A couple of years passed. Health-wise, I recovered and had no residual issues with surgery. Life, eventually, felt good again. Then, I made the decision that it was time to move from the apartment that I had called home for many years. My mother had given me land some years before, but I had not made a decision about what to do with it. The neighborhood kids had been allowed to use it as a park, as a way of keeping them out of the streets. When I soon decided to build my home on that land, I spoke with the neighborhood parents to let them know what was about to happen and why the kids could no longer play on the property. Then, I spoke with the kids, who at that time ranged in age from three to twelve, with one of the youngest, aged three, staring up at me saying, "You're taking our park?" My heart dropped.

But little did I know that with that moment, my life changed for the better.

Upon moving into the neighborhood, the kids would stop to talk to me whenever they saw me. It seemed as if they were determined to know me, whether I wanted them to or not. I became "Momma," "God-Momma," and "Miss Valerie," and they referred to themselves as my kids. Some stayed close, while others were more distant. I learned names, their temperaments, and their educational levels. I helped them prepare for proms, attended graduations, and listened as they told me what I wasn't quite ready to know. It soon became evident that no matter the discussion or my response, they were determined to let me be involved in their lives, and at some point, I discovered that I liked it.

Today, "my kids" are all grown. I have watched them grow into fine young men and women, and I have to admit, I am sometimes amazed at the fact that they really are grown. Throughout the years, I have talked and listened to, fussed at, encouraged, and cried at their stumbles and achievements. All are high school graduates, some enrolled in college, and several opted to get jobs. Several have children of their own. The last and youngest have recently made decisions that I am sure will serve them well. One chose a career in the military, while the other accepted a full football scholarship to a Southern Historically Black College or University. Several stumbled and had brushes with law enforcement before finding their way. They are free to make decisions and choices for themselves, and for the most part, I'm okay with some of the choices that have been made. For the ones I am closest to, it's still in me to want to guide them away from trouble. I want them to see the great opportunities that are available to them, and hopefully, help them understand how choices they make while young can help or hinder their futures. I realize, however, that they are adults, and it is better to be asked into their business than to be asked out! I honor that, until they go too far, of course! That's when "momma mode" kicks in!

It was during my last, and hopefully final, "momma rant" while visiting with some of them that it suddenly occurred to me that I was fussing at adults. I caught myself mid-sentence and apologized to them. I told them I had no right to fuss at them for the choices they make. At that moment, I noticed they all were smiling at me. When I inquired as to why they were smiling, I found that I was set up. They wanted to make me fuss, and I was told, "We don't want you to stop fussing, because we know that you fuss because you love us." Needless to say, I was surprised and teary eyed. They believe I saved them, and because I love them, they made it. The truth of the matter is, they saved me. I'm happy when they visit, and I smile when I receive phone calls that start out with "Hey Momma," "Hey God-Momma," or "Hey Ms. Valerie." They love me, and I love them. Regardless of their stumbles, temporary setbacks, and inevitable successes, they will always be "my kids."

If my plan had worked, my child would have been twenty years old this year. Yes, there are times when I allow myself to wonder if my child would have been a boy or girl, or what he or she would have become. I have even wondered why I was deprived of being a birth mother, and of the opportunity to love someone more than I could possibly love myself—to give love that only a mother can. I haven't allowed myself to linger in that place for long, because I know that I must accept what God has allowed. In my acceptance, I found that although pregnancy was not my fate, and adoption was ultimately not my choice, the opportunity to nurture, guide, and provide life's advice, did and continues to present itself. Coupled with my "inherited" godchildren, I gained a neighborhood of children who filled the space inside me that I believed to be void. I have mothered many – this purpose has been greatly served. I opened myself and my children found me, and if for no other reason than this, I am happily a childless mother.

Valerie C. Jones is the Division Manager for Escambia County Government under the auspices of its Board of County Commissioners, in Pensacola, Florida. She received her Bachelors of Science in Business with an emphasis in Management, and a Masters of Arts in Public Administration from Troy State University. She is an active member of the Zion Hope P.B. Church, The American Planning Association, and Delta Sigma Theta Sorority, Incorporated.

Contact Information:
vcjones408@gmail.com
(850) 384-9937

"SEEING" THE FOREST FOR THE TREES

Yvette D. Bennett

The doctor's voice continues to echo in my head years later. "Yvette, will never be able to have children." I was only thirteen when the doctors gave my mother and me this prognosis, and I was devastated. I was also determined to have my own children, someday, somehow.

When I was in junior high and high school, several girls I knew got pregnant. The teachers, parents, and classmates criticized and shunned them. But all I could think of at the time was how lucky they were to have a baby. I actually felt jealous because they had someone to love him or her unconditionally, their own child. They had something the doctors said I would never have.

The Strength of My Soul

I always wanted my have my own child to love. I wanted someone who would love me unconditionally because I never felt that my own parents loved or wanted me. My parents seemed too wrapped up in their own lives – partying, traveling, and living as single and childless adults. They were unable to adequately care for my brother and me. My father was so wrapped up in his own life that when I was three years old, he walked away and left all of us. I did not see my father again for fourteen years, and I only saw him then because my mother forced him to see me. Of course, being forced to see me didn't make me feel loved. When my father left us, my mother sent my brother and me to live with whoever would keep us. She never explained why she sent us away. It seems as if she didn't mind who took care of us as long as she didn't have to be bothered with us herself. After all, she had her own life to live, and it didn't include my brother or me.

Because I always felt unwanted, I knew at a very early age that I would never be the type of parent that my parents were. I knew that I would give all of the love I had inside of my heart to my child. I would give the love I craved but never received. I didn't know what it felt like to feel loved, wanted, and safe, but I knew that I could learn how to love my child or children more than any parent ever could. Without understanding the impact of being a teenage mother, I tried to convince my high school boyfriend to get me pregnant. I even told him once that I was pregnant just to see how he would react. He was not interested in being a teenage parent; he saw a bright, successful future for himself, and having a child while we were in high school was not part of his plan. But I wanted a child, and it consumed me.

In high school, I met a girl named Chloe. She was a foster child, and when she was thirteen, her mother had given her up to the state. She never told me why she was placed in foster care, but as time went on, I realized why. In the beginning, I took Chloe under my wing because I felt sorry for her. I thought I had it bad being raised by neglectful parents, but I couldn't imagine how she must have felt after her own mother gave her up to the state. I empathized with her because no one loved her either. So, I wanted to be there for her. I understood exactly how she felt.

Chloe complained that her foster father had been trying to molest her. She said his advances were constant, and that she always had to fight him off or hide from him. I was furious, and I encouraged her to report him. She said that she did report him, yet she claimed that nothing was ever done. So, I became her protector and asked my mother and stepfather if they would adopt her. My parents explained that adoption was not a simple process, and that they would have to go through foster parenting classes. After those classes, they would still need approval from state before Chloe could come to live with us. Still, I begged them to take the classes and made them feel guilty for being absentee parents. Finally, they relented. After completing the classes and being approved as foster parents, Chloe came to live with us. She was now my little sister!

I was excited because I thought I finally had the sister I had always wanted. I finally had someone to take care of me and love me. In many ways, I looked at my sister as the child I would never have. Many years later, I would realize that this was the beginning of my Mother Theresa syndrome; I was always trying to save and love someone even when they proved unworthy of my love.

My dream of having a sister quickly turned into a nightmare. Soon, I found out she was a liar. She lied about her previous foster father molesting her. She was mad that she could not get her way in their home, so she lied about him. She was a thief; she stole money from my mother, my brother, and me. She was a manipulator, a con artist, and a user. She was materialistic, selfish, self-serving, and narcissistic. Any boy that I liked, she would sleep with him just to hurt me. She lied about me to other people and would lie to me to make me defend her when she had crossed others. I was shocked and saddened because I couldn't understand why she was such a horrible person. All I ever did was love her and take care of her. And all she ever did in return was repeatedly hurt me. I began to hate her, and I resented her presence in my life.

Later, I found out through a mutual friend that Chloe tried to have sex with my high school sweetheart, the young man I was engaged to and loved. I was enraged, and I confronted her by pulling a knife on her. I was so angry and hurt I wanted to slice her from her navel to her nose. Chloe admitted that she was trying to lure him away from me and offered no explanation. Nothing! I was at a loss. I actually wanted to kill her. To make matters worse, my mother took Chloe's side. My mother tried to shield Chloe from my attacks as I tore through the kitchen with a knife in my hand. I was upset and crazed with anger, like a Tasmanian devil. My stepfather took my side and wanted Chloe out of the house.

But, after the fight, my mother told *me* to leave and to get out of our home. I couldn't believe she was choosing my foster sister over me, her own flesh and blood! My mother had always made me feel unloved and abandoned, and this time was even worse. She was blatantly choosing and supporting the person who had admittedly hurt me, her own child. Immediately, I moved out and Chloe stayed in my parent's home. I moved into my cousin's college dorm room because I had nowhere else to go. And for a whole semester, I was just there, in my cousin's room, with her roommates, depressed, heartbroken, and bitter. I asked God why Chloe came into my life when all she ever did was hurt me. I would constantly forgive her, and she would hurt me over and over.

Almost a year later, I learned that Chloe was pregnant. I was shocked because Chloe was only sixteen. I hadn't had any contact with her, my mother, or my stepfather since I'd moved out of our home and had no idea what was going on inside it. When I learned of her pregnancy, I didn't ask any questions, and I didn't care, because as far as I was concerned, they were no longer my family. A few months later, another friend mentioned that she saw my pregnant foster sister basically living on the streets. Apparently, my stepfather finally kicked her out of the house. My Mother Theresa syndrome kicked in again, and I went looking for her. When I found her, I was stunned. I guessed she was about six months pregnant, but she had no idea of how far along she was because she had not received any prenatal care. I immediately arranged for her to see a doctor, and I paid for everything. During the ultrasound, we learned that she was almost to term; she was eight and a half months pregnant with a baby boy. I was infuriated. She had gone her entire pregnancy without any prenatal care.

Chloe had no desire to be a mother, so she decided to give the baby up for adoption. At that moment, I realized why she had come into my life. She was to give me the child I would never be able to physically have. She and I spent hours discussing my wishes to raise her child as my own, and with some hesitation, she finally agreed. I had to promise that I would never tell him about her because she wanted nothing to do with him. I agreed.

A few weeks later, my son was born, and it was

the happiest day of my life. I was twenty years old and a new mom. I didn't get maternity leave because I had not given birth, so I had to immediately make arrangements for childcare. Chloe refused to watch my son and even refused to help take care of him. She constantly reminded me that he was my baby, not hers. Her reluctance to help me angered me because she was still living with me. I was paying all of the bills and supporting her, but she refused to help; she offered nothing. I wanted to evict her, but she had no money and nowhere to go. My Mother Theresa syndrome kicked in again, and I hired her as a cashier at my job. I hoped earning some money would help her get back on her feet so she could finally move out.

Emotionally, it was difficult having her live with me because she seemed so detached and distant from my son and me. I didn't understand how a woman could give birth to a child and be so disconnected from him. She didn't want to hold him, touch him, or love him. Seeing her lack of concern for my son made me think that she was heartless. Her behavior reminded me about my own parents' lack of concern. Now that I am older, I understand that women are different, and that many variables influence the mother-child connection. Every mother's relationship with her children is not the way I hoped and dreamed my connection to my parents would be. It was a hard lesson to learn.

Eventually, Chloe moved out after getting herself together, and shortly after, I met my now ex-husband. He accepted my son as his own and legally adopted him. My ex-husband and I still yearned to have children of our own, and although the doctor told me it wouldn't be possible, my new husband and I tried anyway. After four years of trying to get pregnant (we tried while we were dating as well), we finally decided to see a fertility specialist. My husband and I truly wanted to have our own biological child. It was wonderful having our son; he was beautiful and such a bundle of joy, but it didn't fill the void we both had to be biological parents. We wanted to experience pregnancy, childbirth, and the connection to a biological child.

The first fertility specialist was not successful. We went to another doctor that a friend had referred me to. The doctor looked over my medical records and said, "If you had come to me first, you would have been pregnant already." He immediately booked me for an exploratory laparoscopy. After the surgery, the doctor informed me that my left fallopian tube was severely damaged and that the right tube was blocked. He was able to unblock the right one, and three weeks later, I was pregnant. Seventeen months after that, I was pregnant again. We gave birth to two beautiful baby girls. Although we continued to try for a short time after my second daughter was born, I was never able to get pregnant again.

Regardless, we were *elated* to finally have the children we were told we would never have. Unfortunately, our joy was short lived when we discovered that my first daughter had Cerebral Palsy and a seizure disorder and would never live a normal life. My second daughter had Lupus and Sjogren's syndrome, and the combination of those two illnesses caused her to develop meningitis every year from age eight until she was almost twenty. There were times when my daughter's meningitis would be so bad that she would have to be put on life support and we didn't think she was going to survive. For years I was very angry with God. I said, "God, why is this happening to us when all we ever wanted were children to love." What I didn't realize at the time was that I had gotten exactly what I had asked for: *my own children to love, all three of them*. It took me years and some growing up to finally see how very blessed I am to have all of my children.

Today, my children are grown. My son is twenty-five, the daughter with Cerebral Palsy is twenty-two, and the daughter with Lupus and Sjogren's syndrome is twenty. They are truly my heart's joy, and they are all doing very well and are healthy for the most part. Although I must admit that I do have regrets in my life, I have never for one second regretted any of my children. There are no words that can express my infinite love and appreciation for having my children in my life. They are my greatest blessings.

Life has dealt many blows to my loved ones and me. My children's father and I divorced when my children were young, but we remained friends. I remember saying to myself, when I finally recovered from my divorce, "If I can get through this, I can handle anything!" I did, and I can! My children and I were sent here to make a difference in people's lives, and we still have a lot to do. The trials I have experienced changed me into a better person and a better mother. My trials helped me to learn, grow, to *appreciate* what I have, and to actually see the forest for the trees. In every trial there is a blessing. On the other side of every storm are our greatest blessings. You just have to be open to seeing and receiving them.

Still, my relationship with my mother is basically nonexistent. We were never able to fully recover from what had happened during my childhood, and I am okay with that. Chloe, my foster sister, has been out of my life now for over twenty years, and I have no desire to know where she is or anything about her ever again. My father and I are trying to build a relationship. My children and I spend time with him, and we are trying to grow together as a family and to mend the brokenness of my childhood.

I know that I will still face hard days. My daughter with Cerebral Palsy still has seizures, but they only occur once or twice a year now, which truly is a blessing. My daughter with Lupus still has flare-ups, but she hasn't had a bout with meningitis for a while. Her flare-ups are now showing up as infections instead of meningitis. Although she still suffers a lot of pain, we are learning to manage her illness with medication.

As long as we walk on this earth, there will be hard days, storms, and trials, but there will also be many more beautifully blessed days. I choose to focus on all of the good things in my life, my many blessings. I choose to share positive energy with everyone I meet. I teach my children to love by being an example of love and light. And I think they are following in my footsteps and spreading love everywhere they go. My children and their love of life make my soul sing because they, too, are able to see the forest from the trees.

Ase'

Yvette D. Bennett has overcome many obstacles in her life that some would feel are designed to break the human spirit. But instead of being broken, Yvette has persevered by conquering many of her goals and is now watching her dreams come true! Yvette holds a Bachelors of Fine Arts in Film from American Intercontinental University in Atlanta, Georgia, where she served as a Media Society President.

As an Asset Manager for Universal Pictures, Yvette is already making her mark in the film industry by working in over fifty short films, commercials, reality shows, documentaries, feature films, and television sports segments as a writer, producer, and director. She has been fortunate enough to work with many industry professionals and celebrities who have assisted her in honing her craft. Currently, Yvette is developing two web series that she has created, along with two feature films and a collection of short films and commercials she has written.

Soon, Yvette will be adding "published author" to her list of accomplishments, which has been her dream since childhood. This is only the beginning for Yvette. She feels that these experiences and opportunities will help to catapult her even closer to achieving everything she has dreamed of and set out to accomplish, making heartfelt, entertaining, inspirational, and quality movies that everyone will enjoy, and writing books that will help to motivate and inspire everyone to live their best life.

Health & Healing

A PERCEIVED HURDLE IS A NOT A HURDLE AT ALL

Colleen Pratt

My mentor once told me that a perceived hurdle is a not a hurdle at all. He also believed that the stronger you are, the less you will perceive hurdles. These axioms are not mere platitudes, and when applied with intention, they can yield astonishing results. Because perceiving and internalizing the hurdles we have to face can be our downfall, and not the hurdle itself. Navigating through life with a fearless and sometimes oblivious indifference to obstacles will not only lead to the success you desire, but it can also ease the stress and angst that exists on the path to getting there.

As a practicing attorney, I find myself in a male-dominated profession, entrenched daily in an environment dominated by male values and attitudes. From law school to being a partner of a firm, I have dealt with insensitive gender jokes, tacit remarks of inferiority, and a general belief that women are weaker than men. But I can state with utmost sincerity that I never once allowed my gender, or any other perceived disadvantage, to be a hurdle. While some would criticize my oblivion as disempowerment, I describe it as freedom – freedom from the mental bondage that perception too often creates.

Your self-assuredness and confidence are your greatest assets! For this reason, my hope is to both inspire and replenish the confidence that often gets chiseled away in our formative years, and sadly, even into middle age. I am here to tell you that it is okay to have blinders on, to block out strife and negativity, until you simply don't think that way. Live life as if you have a right to everything you want, and you will walk with a natural confidence over, around, and through whatever stands in your way. I am not implying that this is an easy task, nor am I naïve to the existence of racism, sexism, ageism, or any other form of discrimination. I am merely encouraging you to control your perception of these real hurdles and fight through them so you can succeed and have the life you want and deserve.

When I reflect on the events in my life, which others would surely define as adversity, I am thankful that I never allowed myself to perceive them that way. Doing so would have created apprehension, fulfilled my own prophecy of failure, and made the roads I traveled bumpier than they should've been. And I have had my fair share of bumps in the road. When I was twenty-nine years old, I was diagnosed with stage IV cancer and was told I had an eighty-five percent chance of dying, even with treatment. But I assure you that this is not a story of self-pity, of my bout with cancer, or how I overcame the odds. This is not a memoir, detailing my story either.

I am writing this because I have a purpose, which is to change your perceptions so you can view challenges differently, and eventually not even recognize when an obstacle is in your path. You will simply step over it as you would naturally take any other step in life. While most stories of cancer survival involve tragedy and then triumph, that's not how my tale begins and ends.

After earning my Bachelors of Arts in Psychology, I had no idea what I wanted to do with my newly acquired knowledge, let alone what to do with the rest of my life. We all know those people who know exactly what they want to do after college. I wasn't one of them. I had all the discipline in the world, but no direction to apply it. Then, one day, on a whim, I decided to go to law school. I was not your typical candidate – I had been a student-athlete, had a marginal grade point average, and did not come from a pedigree of academia. But I never contemplated the difficulty, my aptitude to compete in such a setting, or the likelihood of success. Had I contemplated those potential struggles, self-doubt and a fear of failure would have set in, and I would've eventually convinced myself that I was out of my league. Instead, I just did it. I took the test to get in, applied to various local law schools, and within two months of my decision, I was sitting in a classroom listening to a law professor tell the class that by the end of the program, most of us would not be there.

During law school, I was surrounded mostly by men and students with superior academic resumes, but I was completely (and oddly) unaware of my surroundings, as if I had blinders on. My focus was on the prize, and the prize was passing the Bar exam. It didn't matter that I was outnumbered as a female, or that I was of mixed descent (most people couldn't figure out anyway), or that my college GPA was less than stellar. What mattered was my goal, and I am certain that my obliviousness to what society deems as built-in disadvantages proved to be an asset.

After four years of torment, sleepless nights, and countless case briefings, I finished in the top two percent of the class, received nine Jurisprudence Awards, and passed the California Bar exam on my first attempt. Right out of the gate, I began practicing at a fast-paced, high-volume civil litigation firm. I was in my late twenties at the time, and my life seemed completely on track. I was that prototypical young attorney who drove a shiny black Porsche, polished from head to toe, with a golden smile, and more money than I knew what to do with at that age. There was a price, however, that came along with such a lifestyle, but I was willing to pay it. I worked long, ungodly hours, well into the night, and the stress of deadlines and contentious litigation became the standard of everyday life. I was living the dream, or what I imagined it to be, until I was awakened by one of life's pesky realities.

After practicing for a couple of years and climbing the ladder in the firm, my seemingly charmed life took an abrupt turn after what was supposed to be a routine physical with my doctor. He discovered a 5mm malignant melanoma, and just like that I was transformed from super-lawyer to a patient with stage IV cancer. Even though I made a career of fighting for others, when it came to myself, the gloves came off. When I was told of my meager chance of survival, my very first thought was to drive my car off a cliff and go out pain-free with the thrill and adventure with which I had lived my life. The thought of physically deteriorating while the cancer spread was simply not an option for me. Tears flowed down my face as I called the first person to break the news to – my dad. There was no easy way to tell my father, the only man who has stood by my side through everything in life, that daddy's little girl was faced with one of the most formidable and aggressive cancers, and worse yet, had only a fifteen percent change of surviving. There was no easy way to tell him, so I just blurted it out.

I tried to be strong and hold back my tears, but that battle was quickly lost. I could not stop crying. And when he heard the pain in my voice, the treatment options available, and the unlikelihood of success, he understood exactly why I wanted to plummet off a cliff.

In true fatherly fashion, he supported me, and my wild idea. As an unconventional father who raised me to challenge authority, walk my own path, and never conform, he related to my aversion to western medical treatment and my desire to accelerate the inevitable in thrilling fashion. After the initial shock wore off, reason set in, and the onslaught of medical visits ensued. I was given a treatment plan of chemotherapy and was advised to seek the services of a "life-planner" to plan the final stage of my life. (Frankly, I never knew such a career existed!) Although I railed against chemo, I ultimately succumbed and began treatment as advised. After two weeks of chemotherapy, I lost nearly twenty pounds, had little to no appetite, and suffered every conceivable side effect chemo had to offer. My already petite physique became frail and was riddled with pain. I remember feeling that if the cancer didn't kill me, the treatment would.

So after two agonizing weeks, I pulled the plug on treatment and decided to take my chances with a different approach. I looked into holistic methods of healing, much to the chagrin of my team of doctors. I never doubted my decision to end treatment, and I don't remember ever feeling as if I would not succeed. Failing in this situation had far greater implications than anything else I've ever faced, but I didn't have time to contemplate failure. I kept my eye on the prize, which was to stay alive.

Physically, I began acupuncture treatment targeted to boost my immune system, started an herbal regimen, changed my diet, and began a rigorous exercise program. Metaphysically, I began a process of intense meditation, visualization healing, and insulation from negativity. In addition to eliminating negative people and situations from my life, I stopped watching or reading any news from any media source, ever again. The days of watching countless stories of tragedy, disaster, and misfortune were over for me. I decided that I would not allow the emanation of negativity from the news to affect the positive vibration I vowed to maintain. While some may view this disconnect from local and world events as irresponsible, it was, and still remains, essential to my survival.

At the same time, I began my new physical regimen, which I implemented in easy-to-digest segments – I started a daily health plan, which turned into a monthly, then yearly, routine. Ultimately, this transformed into a way of being. After countless PET scans, CT scans, and blood tests, my ostensibly impulsive plan to end chemotherapy paid off, and the obstacle known as cancer was behind me. It has now been twelve years since my initial diagnosis, and I am healthy, happy, whole, alive, and free.

I could have easily fallen prey to cancer until it was my time to go. I could have gone through the motions and wallowed in my misfortune, but blinders kept me from doing that. I stayed positive and pressed on. I figured I didn't have a choice, much like finishing law school, passing the Bar, or any other challenge I've undertaken in my life. Whether something is tiring or not, I've been programmed to keep my eye on the prize. Because of this, I'm here to tell you that you can do the same. In this life, one thing after another is going to come at you. The question becomes how you will react to what is thrown your way. We are sold the fantasy that some day life's going to be easy, but that's fiction. Life is constantly changing, and the way we perceive it is what makes it easy or difficult.

The beauty is that we get to choose to look at things from either a positive or negative viewpoint. How magnificent it is that nothing and no one can ever take away our perception! It is ours to create, along with our destiny. We are literally the masters of our perceptual destiny. See beyond the challenge, whether you asked for it or not, and whether it is tiring or not. Adversity is tiring. But I am here to tell you that the root of success is to ignore the feeling of being tired, to ignore the perception of being disadvantaged, to ignore people who tell you that you are less than or not good enough, and to turn a blind eye to your perceived hurdles. Don't let challenges slow you down. Instead, make them invisible or step around them. Remember, a perceived hurdle is a not a hurdle at all.

Over the past fourteen years, **Colleen M. Pratt** has practiced law in Southern California with an emphasis on civil litigation. She is known for her tenacity, optimism, dedication, and sensitivity to her clients' needs. Ms. Pratt's high rate of client satisfaction and excellent case results have earned her honors in 2013 and 2015 as Top Lawyers in California and Highest in Ethical Standards & Professional Excellence.

Ms. Pratt received her Bachelors of Arts in Psychology from California State University of Dominguez Hills and attended law school at

Colleen Pratt

Western State University College of Law. At Western, she was Editor of the Law Review and was proud to be a member of the Women's Law Association. During her tenure in law school, she received nine American Jurisprudence awards and ultimately graduated with Cum Laude honors.

Ms. Pratt has handled thousands of cases, and her accomplishments span from the Federal District Court to the California Superior Court, and all the way to the California Court of Appeal. Her watchwords have always been and will continue to be: commitment, dedication, and compassion.

POWERFUL, POWERLESS, DIFFERENTLY EMPOWERED

Dr. Elaine Martin-Hunt

What is he going to say? Clearly something is wrong. Hopefully, it's something that can be easily repaired. Those were the thoughts going through my head on the way to the neurologist's office to get the test results. I had prayed, said positive affirmations, and talked to a therapist, but my anxiety was still very high and my emotions mixed. I had faith that God was in control, but I also knew that my faith only slightly outweighed my fear. That was a pivotal moment along the journey from powerful to powerless, and from powerless to differently empowered.

From a very early age, I had a strong sense of

personal power. That was clearly evident in a particular show of childhood defiance one hot afternoon. It was one of those days when you could see the heat radiating from the asphalt. Like a pint-sized pied piper, I boldly encouraged and led the other six-year-old girls as we paraded through the playground with our blouses blowing open in the hot breeze. It didn't make sense to me that we should not liberate our chests, especially since at that age girls and boys look alike. Why should the boys have the benefit of exposed skin while the girls suffered under the heat of cotton fabric, or even worse some polyester blend? I felt powerful and justified in my actions, although the subsequent spanking I received taught me there was usually a price to pay for defiance.

This playground stand for justice was the beginning of a history of living according to what *I* deemed to be right. That energy of determination flowed throughout my life, from selecting male-dominated classes in high school and college to following my desire to attend seminary. In spite of the obstacles, I managed to excel where some thought I should not be. I learned to balance life as a mechanical designer, quality consultant, or project manager, while at the same time earning degrees in manufacturing engineering technology, a Master of Divinity and a Doctor of Ministry. Somewhere in the course of all of that, I became a pastor for a church and served as a community activist. I was in control. My confidence was high, and I felt as powerful as an African American Wonder Woman. Then life reminded me that even Wonder Woman was vulnerable.

On Labor Day of 1999, I entered the Tour de Town bicycle ride, a long trek through the hilly roads on the north end of Atlanta. The event started early in the cool of the morning, but the comfortable temperature was short lived. As the thermostat indicator increased, my energy level decreased. Despite years of cycling, I could barely make it up the hills, and my feet kept slipping out of the petal stirrups. I felt like some sort of vampire was draining my life-force to stay alive in the light of the sun. Confusion moved in as my strength moved out.

The Tour de Town was just the beginning of a trip from health to disability. Shortly after that ride, I started to feel an uncomfortable tingling sensation down the left side of my body. That was soon accompanied by tripping for no reason, as if my toes had a mind of their own. Then my hands started to shake so badly that I couldn't even think about carrying a cup of hot tea. I remember the day I had to sign signature with an X; I was too sad to cry, even though I was terrified. The slope of deterioration seemed to be dropping off fast, and there were no brakes to stop it. Shortly after, my walking and writing became challenging and my speech became slurred, which devastated me since verbal communication was a critical component of project management, ministry, and activism. Something was happening that I could not understand or control. My life had been hijacked, and I was being driven against my will to an unknown destination.

As my body continued to slip beyond my control, my self-confidence began to decrease. How could I continue to feel powerful when my body was seemingly deteriorating over the course of seven months? It is bad enough when betrayal comes from the outside, but it is even harder to accept your own body turning on you. It was a frightening time in my life. I had no map to tell me the next stop on this unfamiliar and undesired trip. I tried to go to the doctor for a diagnosis and possible cure for whatever saboteur was attacking my body. The office visits were often frustrating because the symptoms were transitory and somehow knew to hide at the sight of a stethoscope. I tried my

The Strength of My Soul

best to describe what I thought it was, but I received no answer that explained what it really was. It seemed like I was losing a fight against an unknown enemy. Soon, though, that adversary would be exposed.

Even though movement was a challenge, I continued to go to work managing projects. But one day, as I was working, the back of my chair suddenly fell off. As I tried to catch myself from falling I aggravated something in my back. The resulting pain led me to a neurologist. That was the appointment that would change my life forever. After I described the tingling, numbness, pain, and weakness that was taking over my body the doctor suggested I get an MRI to see what was going on.

A few days after the imaging, I went back to the doctor to get the results. On my previous visit the doctor and the staff were very jovial and friendly. This time they seemed very subdued and almost somber. The doctor called me into a dimly lit room and put several slides from my MRI up for me to see. All I saw were bright white patches that seemed to rise and glow off of the surface of the film. The white image was all over my brain and cervical spine. I would soon learn that those slides were the portrait of my saboteur, and her name was multiple sclerosis. The glowing areas on my brain were enhanced areas of disease activity. Between my brain and my cervical spines, I had seventeen lesions. The MRI film was the map of the attack on my health.

Multiple sclerosis is an autoimmune disease that attacks the myelin that insulates nerves. The results of this attack are problems with muscle coordination vision, balance, and speech. Such a serious condition was difficult to accept as part of my new reality. That was not the sort of life- long companion I had wanted. The diagnosis sent me into temporary state of shock. Although I had tried to be strong and depend on my faith, it seemed like faith needed a life vest to stay afloat in the river of fear and confusion that flooded my consciousness. I had entered the space many of us visit in times of illness, loss, and unwelcomed life changes, for whatever situation we find ourselves in where we know we have fear, but we can't let it win. We put on a positive face, keep it moving, and lock our fear away to avoid being sucked into a quicksand of negativity. I had to take be positive stance in order to accept such a life-altering diagnosis.

As I looked at the MRI results, I asked the doctor

The Strength of My Soul

to show me a brain that had no lesions. I asked him if anyone ever went from the glowing picture to a view with no enhancement. He told me the devastating news that there was no cure for multiple sclerosis, and that although they would not heal completely, the lesions could go dormant. My response to him was a very firm. There may not have been a cure for MS, but if the best I could hope for was for the damaged areas to go dormant, then that was what I was going to work toward. And, as in everything I do, I was going to depend on God's help in the process.

As soon as I left the doctor's office I did everything I could to help myself. I knew God was on my team when I was blessed to get an opportunity to see one of the best specialists in the world. Although others had to wait four months for an appointment, I was somehow able to see him in three days. When I met with him, we developed a treatment plan of medication, nutrition, exercise, stress management, and prayer. After we reviewed all of the unexplained symptoms I had experienced over the years, the doctor surmised that I had probably had multiple sclerosis for twenty years prior to my diagnosis. He said I had done so well over the years due to my positive attitude, spiritual practice, and exercise. I was encouraged to stay on that path.

Although I was doing everything I could do, there was always a lurking fear that never went away. The fear reminded me of a scene from a movie in which the main character was schizophrenic. He lived his life as a husband and a professor, but imaginary characters were always nearby. As my body continued to change, I had the same fear. Multiple sclerosis and its companions of various forms of disability were the haunting images I had to keep at bay. Every now and then I would imagine a wheelchair with my name on it. As the inventory of changes grew, I began to feel like damaged goods.

I wondered, "What would happen to the dreams I had had for my life?" "Was I going to have to live my life alone?" "Who would want to be in an intimate relationship with someone with a potentially progressive chronic illness?" My body's betrayal left me with an indescribable feeling of powerlessness.

There is a common expression used to empower students or employees: knowledge is power. So when it came to living with unfamiliar and undiagnosed symptoms, life became very unnerving. Not knowing what was happening was like being followed by an unknown imaginary monster that seemed larger and more frightening in the dark; a headache was magnified into a brain tumor, a pulled chest muscle became a pending massive heart attack; any ache or pain was multiplied. Receiving a diagnosis was like turning on the light. When the light finally revealed the identity of my antagonist, I was able to see that although it was a serious chronic condition, multiple sclerosis was not a death sentence. Although it was an unwelcome new reality, the disease was not the end of my life. This knowledge helped to stop the images of my demise, but I had a long road ahead of me of figuring out how to live with my new knowledge.

Adjusting to the limitations that accompanied multiple sclerosis was not easy. There were many sad moments when I reflected on how life used to be. I would watch people do things as simple as run up or down the steps and reflect on how I had taken walking and climbing stairs for granted. I would see cyclists on the road on Saturday mornings and remember what it was like to tuck down and feel the wind in my face as I coasted down a hill or traveled thirty or forty miles under my own power. When I realized I had lost my ability to deliver sermons in a regular "Black preaching" style, I thought I would never again be able to use the gift God had given me. In the past I could study a text, write a mind map, and deliver a powerful and meaningful message. With multiple sclerosis, I could not trust my memory to stay on track and didn't have the abdominal strength to project. It felt like many of the things that defined me were slipping away.

I read a card once that said, "It's never too late to be what you could have been." That statement was not totally true. For some of us there are abilities and realities we will never regain. That does not mean life is not valuable or meaningful. It just leads us to a different truth, which is that it's never too late to be what God intended you to be. I did not choose a path for my life that included multiple sclerosis, but it became part of my reality anyway. For years, I felt sadness over the loss of my ability to realize the dreams I had designed. Once I realized that I had a right and a reason to mourn the loss of those abilities, I embraced the grieving process and consciously went through the steps of disbelief, anger, guilt, and acceptance. I was then able to get to the final step of reorienting my life.

As I readjusted my rearview mirror, I could see

that I never really lost my power. The difficulties that arose actually exposed my true strength. I had juggled the duality of fear and determination and succeeded. It was powerful for me to go through treatments that included giving myself a weekly injection with a needle that was 1 ¼-inch long. It was courageous to go through a year of chemotherapy to try to address the remaining active lesions. It was amazing to still be able to work full time, to pastor a church, and to finish a doctorate degree while coming to terms with a difficult diagnosis. What kind of powerless person would have been able to do that?

My former understanding of power seems weak compared to what I know now. In the past, I might have defined power as the ability to have and be the best on the surface, where others could see and agree with my egocentric sense of achievement. Now, however, I have a greater understanding. Rather than thinking I have the power to design and live my life according to my own rule, I have gained a greater type of authority that humility has unleashed. This humility comes from the awareness that I am not in control of everything that happens in my life. The authority comes from knowing that I have a power within me that I call God, who can help me tap into the

Dr. Elaine Martin-Hunt

ability to adjust and start over.

Things have changed. I do not preach the same way I used to, but I have gained a softer style that enables me to reach a much more diverse audience. I do not ride for miles on my bike, but I can ride a few miles and work out at a gym in the morning. I still cannot dance, but I can chuckle at the truth that I was never a good dancer anyway. Walking is not as smooth as it once was, but I can use a cane and will always remember what one of the young people at my church said: "Rev. Kathi, it's okay that you need to use a cane, but make sure you get a cute cane rather than one that looks like a hook." At the advice of that young man, I have a pretty impressive collection of canes for every occasion. I was also blessed to discover that my fear of spending life alone was unfounded. As I learned to love and accept me, I became lovable as well. Today, I have an awesome wife and phenomenal daughter who love me just as I am.

Ministry is still a central part of my purpose. I have been able to birth a creative type of ministry that brings persons together in an unconventional setting to build bridges of community while enjoying a relaxing atmosphere of music, art, and conversation. This new ministry reaches and draws in persons who would normally only attend a church for weddings and funerals. On an individual level, I work with people one-on-one as a spiritual coach to accompany them on their divine journey or to help them navigate the river of chronic illness. I am also open to leading a congregation, but this time with a more refined and humble understanding of life's ups, downs, opportunities, and possibilities.

The journey from powerful to powerless, and from powerless to differently empowered has not been easy, but it has been beneficial. The challenges helped stretch me far beyond what I thought I could bear. The joys have given me an appreciation for each day and the courage to live outside of my comfort zone. I would be lying if I said there is no fear in me; it still lurks in the shadows. The more impactful force that keeps me moving, however, is love. I find authentic, life-enhancing power in love for myself, love for God, love for my family, and the awareness that God loves and is with me, just as I am.

Dr. Elaine Martin-Hunt

Elaine Martin-Hunt is a speaker, preacher, and spiritual guide with over twenty years of experience serving the community through ministry and community activism. She is a former pastor of First Immanuel A.M.E. Church and the founder of God, Self, and Neighbor Ministries, both of which are in the Atlanta metropolitan area. In addition, she is the founder and spiritual director of an alternative ministry, The Interactive Faith Café, and the owner of You Can Still Believe, LLC, which offers life and spiritual coaching.

Dr. Martin-Hunt received a Bachelors of Science in Manufacturing Engineering Technology, a Master of Divinity from of The Interdenominational Theological Center in Atlanta, Georgia, and a Doctor of Ministry from Columbia Theological Seminary in Decatur, Georgia. She has served on numerous panels and conducted workshops at churches, colleges, organizations, radio, and television.

Dr. Martin-Hunt lives with her wife and daughter and three four-legged friends in Stone Mountain, Georgia.

ME, MOM, AND DEMENTIA

Quentella Morris

In 2004, my mother died at the age of ninety-eight after living with me for eleven years. When she reached the age of ninety-five, she started to show signs of dementia. She began to forget simple things like where she put her glasses or where she put the newspaper that she so loved to read. I noticed that she was beginning to deteriorate more and more each year. When she reached her ninety-eighth birthday in October, her condition rapidly declined.

During this decline, my focus was not on my feelings; my main concern was my mother and how she felt about slowly losing her memory. In the beginning, she was aware that she was having trouble remembering; at first, she would make fun of it. She had a good sense of humor. But the more she deteriorated, the more frustrated she became and the more she struggled. Doing simple things like bathing herself, dressing herself, making her bed and reading became challenging. Seeing her struggle with these simple tasks was difficult, and I felt helpless and sad. I knew that there was nothing that I could do but pray.

During her times of lucidity, I encouraged her, talked with her, and prayed with her. Even though our roles changed and I was now her caregiver, I never forgot that she was still my mother. She was the parent, and it was my job as her daughter to encourage her to continue to do as much for herself as she could. I wanted her to feel independent. You see, I believed that since she had taken care of me, it was time for me to take care of her, like a daughter should. So I would never tell her that what she was doing something wrong when she was trying to do something right. I remember when she put on her dress inside out. Since we weren't leaving the house, I did not try to change it because she was very content with the way it was.

Mom was a praying woman. She would sit in her room praying, singing, and reading her Bible. Her prayer was "God, don't let me a burden to my daughter. If I can no longer take care of myself and lose my ability to walk, just take me on home." I felt that whatever happened, with God's help, I would not let her feel that she was being a burden to me. The Lord heard her prayer, because she died four weeks after she lost her ability to walk.

As Mom's health declined further, she would talk about her life and relive incidents from her youth. She remembered the names of some of her relatives who had long-since passed away. In fact, one day when she wanted to talk to her long-lost cousin Rebecca, I would not give her the telephone number because it was not available. She took the telephone directory and looked for the number herself. When she could not find it, she became very frustrated. When I told her that Rebecca was dead and explained why she would not find her name in a Texas directory, she told me that I did not know what I was talking about. She continued to look, but she eventually gave up. She also believed that one of her cousins lived around the corner from my house and wanted me to take her to see her. When I refused, she said that she would walk instead, by herself.

My mother loved to walk, even though she had to

use a cane to keep from falling. Sometimes she would forget it or tell me that she didn't need it anymore. She was blessed in that when she did fall, she did not seriously injure herself. Mom's walking became so frequent that I had to put childproof grips on the doorknobs because she would open the door and go outside by herself. The childproof grips really frustrated her, but they did not necessarily keep her from leaving alone. She would tell me to open the door, and I would ask her where she was going. Most of the time, she would say that she was going home. Sometimes she didn't realize that she was already home. Sometimes, I would open the door and watch her walk. I would not do this as often as she wanted me to because she would go out, come right back in, and then decide that she wanted to go back out again. This was, of course, very frustrating to me.

One day, she kept trying to open the door and telling me to let her out. At first, her insistence bothered me because I knew she didn't really know what she wanted to do. She would bang on the door and persist until I got so frustrated that I would let her out. Once out, she would walk half a block and get so tired that she could not walk back to my house. I would always walk behind her to make sure she was safe, and I usually had her wheelchair available for her to use to return home.

Sometimes I would stay up all night watching her because she refused to get in bed and go to sleep. For some reason, at nighttime, she needed to turn on the lights so she could see. She would also come into my bedroom looking for things that she had misplaced, all while calling my name. On one particular night, she decided she wanted to go outside, but she could not find the door. She started banging on the windows, messing up my window blinds, yelling, "Let me out! Let me out!" She went from window to window. At first I was afraid for her. Then, I just stood back and watched, because I did not want her to hurt her or me.

This time was exhausting for me, and I frequently became upset. Many times I felt like screaming at her, but I restrained myself. I figured that when she found out she couldn't leave, she would settle down. It took her fifteen minutes to realize that she could not get out through the windows. In the morning, she didn't remember what she had done, even when I reminded her of it. Sometimes, she would tell me that I did not know what I was talking about. I learned early on not to argue with her in those cases, because I would never win.

Before her health declined, Mom loved to cook. She would do all of the cooking for the family because she thought I didn't know how to cook well. When I did cook, she would eat my food, but always stated that she could do better. Even though she enjoyed cooking, I had to limit her cooking time because she would leave the stove on or burn the food. I also kept my knives dull because I did not want her to cut herself. When Mom tried to clean up after cooking, she would sometimes forget what she was doing and leave the faucet running. She sometimes plugged up the sinks, causing flooding in her bathroom and the kitchen.

Mom also loved a clean house. Her room and bathroom were always clean. When she could no longer clean her room, I would do it for her because I knew how much she needed cleanliness. When dishes were left in the sink, she would wash them and then complain that we did not keep our kitchen clean enough. She washed dishes for as long as she could because we never wanted her to stop trying. When she could help with the chores, she felt valued. Sometimes, the dishes would have to be rewashed. Of course, we rewashed them when she wasn't looking.

Although my mother's dementia was difficult for her and for me, my mother taught me many things during this time. She continued to pray, read her Bible, and sing. When things got tough for her, she would always whisper a prayer. She would praise God for the little things. Don't get me wrong, there were times when I became very frustrated or angry because I could do nothing about her illness. At times, I wanted to give up and place her in an assisted-living facility. But I remembered the promise we, the family, made to our dad on his deathbed: to care for Mom and never place her in a nursing home. That was a promise I was determined to keep as long as I could.

There were times when I wanted to argue with her, but arguing didn't do her or me any good because she did not understand why I was concerned. One particular incident comes to mind in which she accused my husband of stealing her money. We would allot her a portion of her money for church tithes and offerings, or for when she went shopping with me. If she saw something she wanted, she could buy it with her own money. When she accused my husband of stealing, I would tell her that he never even went into the room she kept her money in. She called me a liar. Of course, my husband was offended. I tried to calm him down, reminding him of her mental condition. Still, the lack of trust hurt both of us, and after my mother calmed down, I went into her room and into one of her hiding places, and found the money. She never did apologize.

Mom's illness also taught me patience. For years I prayed to God for patience, and this God- given patience helped me deal with my mother's illness. There were times when I had to go into my bathroom and cry to avoid raising my voice to her. Deep inside, I wanted to just scream. Instead, God gave me a song to sing, and I would find peace through song. God is a good God, and through His goodness, I was able to take some of the verbal abuse from my mother.

Another thing my mother taught me throughout her life was to be faithful to God. That meant going to church, working in the church, paying my tithes, giving my offerings, reading my Bible, praising God, and meeting Him in prayer. It did not matter how she felt; when it came time for church, she never missed an opportunity to attend. Sometimes she would be ready before I was, and other times I had to wait for her. One Sunday, she was not doing well, but she wanted to go to church so I helped her get dressed. At that point, it was necessary for her to use her wheelchair, but she didn't like it, especially when she went into a church building. But since she needed to go, she accepted the chair and had a good time once we were there.

I know I am a better person for taking care of my mother. Because of her, I am at peace with myself, and I really feel good about the way I took care of her. I thought I had peace before, but now I am more tolerant of others. I know now how to let things go. I know my limitations. I know when to listen, when to speak, when to confront, and when to back down. I also learned that I did not know as much about myself as I thought I did.

I thank God for my mother and for everything she taught me during her illness. It strengthened my resolve in the Lord and increased my understanding of what people go through when dealing with their illnesses, mentally, physically, and spiritually. Every day, I thank God for my mother. I miss her, and I think about her often. She encouraged me to take some time for myself, and now, I am.

My prayer: Lord, I thank you for giving me the

strength to take one day at a time. Look on the caregivers and give them the strength to make it on a daily basis. Help them to realize that they are doing a special service for you. Amen.

Quentella Morris holds a Bachelors of Arts in Sociology, a Masters of Arts in Educational Administration, a Masters of Science in Counseling, and a Psy. D in Psychology. She is the co- owner of Morris and Siler Consultants, LLC, a practice dedicated to providing psychotherapy and counseling support to individuals, couples, and groups.

Her areas of expertise are divorce, marriage, family, pre-marital, Christian, adolescent, children, art and sand tray, stress management, Shiatsu, parenting workshops, and domestic violence (both the perpetrator and the victim). She also works closely with patients who suffer from depression and anxiety.

Even as a retired schoolteacher and principal, Quentella continues to dedicate her life to guiding and supporting young people. She is actively involved in her church and volunteers in the following departments: Sunday school, children's church, vacation Bible school, tutoring, and recreational activities.

Quentella is also a published author of two books, *Echoes from the Old Testament*, and *Wisdom for Teens*.

THE SUMMER OF CRAZY

Shannon Lagasse

Just three weeks before school was out for summer, my parents kidnapped me and forced me into a mental hospital.

I had just arrived home from school and was settling into my moon chair (the same one I'm writing in right now) to do my homework when I heard a car pull into the driveway. Odd, I thought. Daddy and Steppy are already home. When I looked out the window, I saw my mom's Camry and both her and Dave climbing out of it. They walked in the front door and asked my dad, who did not sound shocked at all by their sudden appearance, "Where is she?" Then, they walked down the hallway from the living room to my bedroom. When they appeared in my doorway, I was a bit confused. Why were they here? Was this an intervention or something?

"Pack your bags," they said. "You're going with us." Now I really did not like where this was going. After all, I had just moved to my dad's and wasn't thrilled with the notion of spending time at my mom's. So I packed an overnight bag, grabbed my laptop, and hugged my other parents goodbye while Mom and Dave led me out of the house. They didn't say anything on the entire forty-five-minute drive back to New Hampshire, which really irked me, as I was still wondering what was up.

When the car stopped, I realized we weren't at my mom's house at all. There was sign on the building on the door that read, "Hampstead Hospital."

"You're here to meet with a psychiatrist," my parents told me.

Um, okay, I thought. Wouldn't it just have been easier to send me here after school instead of making me drive all the way to Plum Island and back?

I walked into the therapist's office and sat down on the rather uncomfortable leather sofa to answer her questions.

"Shannon," she said, "do you know why you're here?"

"Yeah," I said. "Because I'm fucked up, have anorexia, and my parents want me to get better."

"Okay. Do you know where you are?"

"Not really. They just told me I'm here to talk to the psychiatrist so I can get help."

"Okay, honey. You're at Hampstead Hospital. This is an in-patient psychiatric facility. Your parents have registered you to join us for a few days in the young adults ward, where we can keep track of you and where you can get the help you need."

I could've died from embarrassment. I had an *eating disorder*, not mental problems! I couldn't be here. I didn't belong here. And I didn't have a few days to spare for shootin' the shit with some crazies. Just tomorrow I was due to present a speech to the student body so I could be the next student liaison to the school board! How was I supposed to do that from the hospital?

So I did what I did best – I ran away.

I stood up and walked right out the front door, surprised that no one even tried to stop me. I started walking down the road, not entirely sure of where I'd go, but knowing I couldn't stay *there*.

A car pulled up alongside me, on the other side of the road. Dave leaned his head out the window. "Shannon," he said, "get in the car."

"No."

"Shannon, this is going to be so much easier for everyone if you just get in the car."

"No!" And then I started to run, cutting down a side road, looking for a place, any place, to hide. I felt like a fugitive on the run from the law. I was humiliated. Who knew who was out there watching me, watching us, while my parents chased me down so they could lock me up? I have nightmares about it to this day.

I ended up turning down a side street into a beautiful neighborhood filled with idyllic houses, homes that probably housed families much more sane and normal than mine. I heard a car behind me and jumped into the hedges, curling up into the fetal position. This is where Dave found me, picked me up, and forced me into the car, returning me to my new home at Hampstead Hospital. He dragged me into the building with me fighting every step of the way, holding onto the glass doors, kicking, screaming, throwing my arms around in the air, looking every part the crazy my parents and the administrative staff thought I was.

Then, they checked me into the hospital, and a nurse escorted me to the young adult's wing. I ignored my parent's goodbyes, resenting them with every ounce of my being for doing this to me, for locking me up like some crazy person. The attendant took me into a room and strip-searched me, pulling the shoelaces out of my shoes, taking my earrings away from me, checking my tongue and belly button for any piercings I could use to stab myself or someone else. They left my computer with my parents, as well as my spiral bound notebooks, lest I should remove the binding and choke myself with it, which, when it dawned upon me where I was and what was happening, seemed like a really appealing option.

That night, when I went to brush my teeth, I found that the bathrooms had no mirrors. When I asked the nurse why, she said that they couldn't take any chances with materials that someone could use to hurt themselves or others. Apparently, a girl had once broken the mirror with her fist and used it to cut herself, at which point they removed all the mirrors from the bathrooms.

What kind of a place had my parents committed me to? And whom was I going to meet in the morning when everyone in the wing was awake?

The next morning, when I came out into the common area by the bathrooms, I saw a bunch of young people. They looked pretty normal, except for this heavy girl with cuts all over her arms and face. Hesitantly, I sat down at one of the tables.

"What are you here for?" the girl next to me asked.

"Because my parents are jerks," I replied.

"But really," she pressed. "What did you do? Cut yourself? Take pills?"

"I'm just anorexic," I said.

The girl seemed disappointed.

The kids around the table started to introduce themselves, telling me their names, ages, and reasons they were committed to the hospital. There was a little girl, about nine years old, who was there for depression. The girl next to me had tried to kill herself. The guy across the table was from a foster home and had anger management issues that got him kicked out and locked up. The big girl with the cuts was there for cutting and raging outbursts that I would later become all too familiar with.

I didn't belong there. All I had was an eating disorder. I wasn't crazy or anything. I wasn't hurting anyone.

And that's the thing about eating disorders: while they're categorized by mental illness, they're so difficult for most people to understand. Because while we've all been a bit depressed or anxious at times, it just seems incomprehensible that you'd want to deprive yourself of food all day. When we look at the word "anorexia," it means "loss of appetite." But we don't specify the appetite. It's not that I didn't feel hungry during the day. It's not that I didn't want to eat or didn't salivate thinking of my favorite foods – I felt like I couldn't eat. Not eating was my way of being in control. It was my way of numbing the pain of trying to be perfect all the time, and despite what seemed like a lot of external success, I never felt good enough.

Anorexia was a way of slowly killing myself. It was a way to put me out of my misery and distract me from my pain. And that doesn't make sense to most people. Why would you hurt yourself more so you could hurt less? But in a twisted way, it made complete sense to me: I could feel the pain of hunger, or I could feel the pain of overwhelm, of fear, of anger, of hurt, of rejection, of abandonment, and of so many other things whose weight seemed to bear down on my body.

So it was symbolic that I was losing weight. If I could lose weight, if I could be lighter, maybe then I wouldn't feel so heavy. Maybe then I wouldn't feel so burdened and encumbered by life. That's why I think it's not about trying to fully understand eating disorders, but rather about drawing parallels to other conditions and making analogies to more common life circumstances so we can at least begin to understand, and thus have some more compassion for, eating disorders. I don't expect anyone who hasn't struggled with an eating disorder to get what it's like to feel so bogged down by reality, but if I can give you a glimpse or an inkling of what it's like by relating it to your own life, I've done my job, and maybe I'll finally be able to sleep at night.

The second time I ended up at Hampstead Hospital, I called the cops on myself.

I was at my dad's house one night, and we were having an argument about God knows what – probably our millionth argument to date, usually stemming from my dad's inability to connect and relate with what was going on with me.

The result of our argument was my teetering on the edge of my safe zone, my mind drifting into two distinct possibilities for what I'd do next: take the car and drive away or take the car and run it off the road.

In that moment, I knew I couldn't be at home anymore, because if I were I'd do something stupid. I'd do something I'd regret – if I even lived to regret it.

So I made a split decision and called 911.

The cops arrived with an ambulance. I greeted them at the back door. My parents ran upstairs after hearing the sirens in the yard, clueless as to what was going on.

They looked at me. "Shannon, why are the cops here?"

I stared them down. "Because I don't feel safe, and they're going to take me away."

They asked me why I didn't tell them, why I would call the cops instead of letting them know that I needed to get away, why I would waste the money on an ambulance when they could drive me to the hospital themselves. But before I could answer, before I could convey to my parents exactly how scared I was of what they might say to me, how they invalidated my feelings, brushing them off as just another silly thing my eating disorder concocted, the medics started to ask me questions, pulling me away from my parents. Then, they strapped me onto a stretcher.

As they loaded me onto the ambulance, I felt relief start to settle in. I was on my way to safety. I was about to be reunited with the only people in the world who understood me, the other kids who knew what it was like to struggle, to want to hurt themselves, to feel unsafe around their families, the very people who were supposed to love them, protect them, and care about them the most.

On the way to the ER, the EMTs questioned me. As was usually the case, the very compassionate medics asked why a girl like me would want to end her life and throw it all away. While it was very sweet of them to ask, it just deepened the feeling I had that no one would ever understand me outside of that mental hospital. How could these people not see I was dying inside already? What did it matter if I was killing myself on the outside? How could they not see the pain I suffered day in and day out? They didn't know what it was like to hear voices in your head telling you you're not good enough, forcing you to starve, to exercise, to do anything and everything you could to be better, all so that maybe someday you'd be good enough, even when you knew you never would be. You know things are a little bit off in your life when you feel more at home in a psychiatric facility with girls who tear off their skin and break open windows with dresser drawers than while living with your family.

After my second stay in the young adult's quadrant, I decided I'd rather stay in there with all the other crazy people than go home to the people who constantly harped on me and badgered me with questions without ever stopping to actually listen for the answer. At least in the hospital people understood me; they not only listened to me, but they *heard* me.

Now, let me just get on my soapbox for a second here. There's something to say for being in a place where everyone has no choice but to admit that they'd fucked up at least a little bit. There's something liberating about baring all your flaws and insecurities to strangers who aren't afraid to share their own. Whether they had overdosed on pills, cut their wrists, or thrown Godzilla-like temper tantrums in their foster homes, all of those kids had a story to tell, and they weren't ashamed to share it. After all, how often are we given the opportunity to open the doors and shine a light on all of our deepest, darkest secrets? In a world that shuns imperfection, living in a place full of it was a blessing.

So often, in the "outside world," we put a wall, a barrier, around our feelings and our experiences. We hide behind these walls and pretend that we are faultless, flawless beings, when, deep down, we feel hurt, broken, and empty. We feel pain we have no idea how to express, because when all other people hide behind their masks of perfection, we feel vulnerable even thinking about removing our own.

I'll jump off my soapbox now.

That's why when I found myself in the car heading home with my father just a few days after my arrival at the hospital, I felt like someone had taken away my rock, my security blanket, my real support team. As we sped down the highway back to the beach house, and my dad asked me what it was going to take for me to get better, I was reminded of just how unsupported I felt in my real life outside of the hospital. I tried to explain to him what I hope this book explains to you: how an eating disorder works, what my thoughts were like, how difficult it was just to make it through the day, constantly having to battle my own mind, which was torn between hurting myself and wanting to recover.

Since I was in a moving car, hurtling down the interstate at seventy miles an hour, I had no way to escape and no way to avoid his questions or the sideways looks. And somewhere in that twisted and screwed up mind of mine, I got so overwhelmed that I could not think straight. I reverted to my primitive self, the part in me that is like the part in us all that, when hurt, wants to strike back, even if the pain is not physical.

That is how I ended up punching my dad square in the arm.

Of course, I just wanted him to stop. Stop talking. Stop asking questions. Stop not understanding. Stop thinking it was easy to just eat. Stop reminding me of just how much I was fucking up everyone else's life along with my own. Nevertheless, he was pissed. I unbuckled my seatbelt and cowered in the small space underneath the glove compartment and in front of my seat. He yelled at me to get my ass out of there and back onto the chair before he turned the car around and brought me back to the hospital. I dared him to.

The thing is, we've all struggled with something in our lives. Whether it was a mental illness, an eating disorder, a health issue, abuse, or what-have-you, we've all been through the ringer once or twice. What I'm offering you is an opportunity to share *your* truth so you can set others free, so we might all feel comfortable opening up and being our authentic selves. So many of us are hiding from the world because we are afraid of others seeing our pain. But this is the greatest cause of disconnect in our society and in our world. We have become so preoccupied with keeping up appearances that we completely miss out on the opportunity to get to know one another deeply, personally, and fully, wounds and all.

Let this be a call to you to open your heart and share your story with others, a call for compassion through understanding. Because the more we share, the more we relate. And the more we relate, the closer we grow together. And the closer we grow together, the more we find peace. Isn't that what we're all really looking for, connection, peace, and compassion?

Here's to you on your hero's journey. May it be full of revelation, connection, and inspiration to explore greater heights fearlessly.

Shannon Lagasse is the founder of Hunger for Happiness, a business dedicated to changing the way women relate to themselves, their bodies, and the world around them. She is also a recovered anorexic, bulimic, and binge eater turned health coach whose message is one of self-love and self-compassion in the healing and recovery process, whether from an eating disorder or emotional eating. Shannon inspires women worldwide through her writing, coaching, and speaking.

Visit Shannon online or book her to speak at www.HungerforHappiness.com.

SLOWLY LOSING MOM

Sonia Ventura

When she called my name again, it was the third time in less than twenty minutes. I thought I would explode from irritation. I thought, "What does she want now?" I walked into the living room, where she was sitting on the couch, the same spot that she had called me the other two times. And just like those other times, she turned to me and repeated exactly the same statement: "Sonia, make sure you get the clothes out of the dryer." I wanted to yell. I couldn't believe that she called me into the room to talk about the clothes again. I had already, less than an hour ago, retrieved the last load of clothes from the dryer, and we had folded them together. Why is she asking me about the clothes again?

At that moment, a sense of fear filled me, a sense

of dread. Is there something wrong with Mom? I suspected something was off, that something was amiss. I'm not sure where my suspicion came from, because that day wasn't the first time Mom had repeated requests or statements to me. Other times, she repeated herself and made me wonder what was happening to her. But for some reason, this was the first time her constant questioning felt different. And at that exact moment, I realized it was the first time she also recognized that something wasn't right. The fear in her eyes sent chills up my spine. Even though we didn't want to admit it, the signs and the diagnosis were inevitable. She was having problems remembering, and she knew it.

My mother was born in Puerto Rico under less than happy circumstances. She was adopted, but she had no birth certificate issued, so we don't know the exact details of her birth. We know the names of her adoptive parents, her age, and the appropriate place of her birth. But that's it. We are grateful that we know even that much, because without those details, we wouldn't have had the information required for medical care.

Without fully knowing English, Mom moved to New York and worked in a cosmetics factory. She got married, although not happily, and my two sisters and my brother, then had me last. We were her world, and she endlessly loved and nurtured us. I believe Mom tried to give us the love that she had never received.

When my Papi left, we moved to Ohio. Mom had heard that Ford was hiring women to work in the factory, so she moved to give us a better life. Even though she was petite, somewhat shy, and quiet, Mom worked hard to ensure that we had everything we needed. Working on the assembly was grueling; it was labor-intensive work, but Mom persevered. It was also difficult for her because women were not readily accepted in the factories, and of course, being Latina in Ohio was isolating. Without much support on the job and less support from the neighbors, we made it. Mom made sure we had what we needed, even if it meant that she had to borrow money. She was my "s-hero."

My mother had done so much good others and me that I felt it was so unfair for her to lose her memory at such a young age. She was young; she was only 59 when she was diagnosed with Dementia/Alzheimer's. It was also unfair because she had never had the opportunity to live or fully enjoy her life. She had worked her whole life, and now that she was retired, it seemed cruel that she would never have a chance to relax and appreciate life. Honestly, that is what I regret the most – Mom not being able to enjoy her life, especially since she made so many sacrifices for us.

I became Mom's primary caregiver when she turned sixty-six. At that point, it was impossible for her to take care of herself. She could not cook, could not manage her money, could not take care of her home, and could not drive. There were a few times when the Ohio state police contacted us because Mom had driven some place and gotten lost. She could not remember how to get home, and sometimes she couldn't remember who she was. That was enough for me. I went to Ohio, packed up her apartment, and moved her to Atlanta with me.

Initially, Mom was resistant to the move, but I did everything I could to help her adjust. I even brought her furniture down from Ohio so she could have a few familiar things. I did my best to care for her, but it was also difficult, especially since I was going to school full time and working full time. When taking care of Mom became overwhelming, I hired a kind lady to watch her while I worked. I didn't care what it took or how expensive it was; I was going to care for her and shower her with the same love she gave to me.

Even though my mother no longer knows my name or recognizes my face, I still believe that there is a piece of her inside that knows me, and all of her family. It does not bother me at all that she mixes up her information and can't verbalize her feelings. It does not even upset me that she goes in and out of lucidity. Her smile speaks to me and provides the comfort I so desperately need.

What am I feeling? To try to explain what a loved one goes through dealing with a parent with Alzheimer's is really simply impossible. Honestly, I don't believe anybody can fully convey what it feels like; seeing your parent decline right before your eyes is simply painful. It is emotionally, spiritually, and physically excruciating. It is a pain that I have never felt before, one I cannot fully comprehend. All I can say is that seeing Mom deteriorating constantly makes my soul ache.

I experienced every stage and phase of grief as I tried to wrap my mind around my mother's illness. I have tried my best to understand what she must be feeling, too; I can't even imagine what she must have felt when she realized that her memory was fading, and that one day she would no longer remember anything at all. But what I can admit is that I was angry, sad, and anxious, I mostly felt alone. I was scared, for me and, most importantly, for her.

What I can also say is that you lose a part of yourself when you become a caretaker because your life now becomes your parent's life. I can share that it's difficult to explain to someone who has never dealt with a parent with Alzheimer's that you are more than willing to give up your own life to take care of your mother. All I can say is that I remember all the sacrifices my mother made for my siblings and me. I remember the long hours she spent in the Ford car plant, the cold mornings she left for work, the discrimination that she endured being a woman in a male-dominated industry, and the isolation she felt being a Latina with a noticeable accent in Ohio. My mother endured so much for me, and as a result I wanted to care for her. I wanted to repay her. And I knew I had to reciprocate all of the sacrifices that she had made for me.

People always ask me how do I do it, how I deal with seeing my beloved mother wither away right before my eyes. My response is, and will always be, that I have God. I am fully aware that I cannot deal with any of my part of my mother's illness without His guidance and love. Thankfully, God has a way of allowing me to see things in a very different perspective, and that perspective is what grounds me despite my pain.

Always remember you will need God. You will need Him for help and to cry out to, as He will be the only one who truly understands what you are going through. When a loved one is diagnosed with a debilitating disease, trust me, you will want to find Him as soon as possible. I also coped with this dreaded disease through prayer, and boy did I pray. I knew immediately that once I found out my mother was ill I would not be able to handle her diagnosis without a spiritual support system. Through my spiritual support system, I have learned how to continue loving myself and caring for myself. I have learned that talking, crying, and finding a way to express my feelings is liberating. My support system has shown me that I am doing the right thing by loving my mother, and that my sacrifice is worth it.

Once I established a spiritual support system, I set myself up with a personal support system. Without my close friends, I would never have made it through this painful journey. Multiple times, when I needed to decompress from the pressure and pain of witnessing my mother's decline, my friends have shown up and have allowed me to take mental health breaks. When my friends sit with my mother, they give me the opportunity to keep some of my own life. For those friends, and especially for God, I am most grateful.

It is well worth the effort to see that my mother is comfortable, safe, and cared for. I know I will not come out of this experience the same person that I was going into it. I do know that I will be a better person because of the experience; nobody who experiences Alzheimer's stays the same. Without Alzheimer's, I could never feel so ecstatic and tickled as I do when my beloved mother chooses to ever so briefly send me a smile. My mother's Alzheimer's has taught me the authentic meaning of unconditional love and unspeakable joy. I love her, no matter what.

Unfortunately, the disease slowly took over her body and I could no longer take care of her because she needed twenty-four hour support. As a family, we decided that it was best for her to move to Ohio to live with my sister. It was an agonizing decision for me, but I knew that my sister had friends, support, and a church family that could provide the support I didn't have. Reluctantly, and tearfully, Mom left me, and I plunged into a depression. I knew that not only was Mom leaving Georgia, but her memory was leaving, too. Would Mom remember me? Would Mom know my voice? How would I handle Mom not knowing me? Trust me, there were many sleepless, tearful nights in which I tried to make peace with Mom's absence and her illness.

Today, Mom is seventy-three and is slowly but surely fading away. She is now confined to a nursing home, and it takes longer and longer for her to respond to stimuli. I know what that longer response means, even though I wish I didn't. After fourteen years of this dreaded disease, Mom has lost her capacity to communicate, walk, sometimes swallow, or share in her own way. She has lost her ability to use cutlery, feed herself, or comb her hair. She has lost much, so much that it is sometimes too painful to watch her.

It is so astonishingly brutal and torturous to watch someone who was an excellent mother and so full of life be cut away little by little by this dreadful disease. Thankfully, though, Mom has not lost her ability to smile, laugh, and sing. Even if I don't know the song and cannot understand the words, Mom's singing brings me joy. Her singing comforts me, even though in many ways I am inconsolable. I miss her; I miss my mom.

So what do I now know for sure? I know to love deeply and share generously. Never miss an opportunity to express love to your parents, or anybody you love. Mom knew that I loved her, and she knows I love her now, because I always told her and showed her. Don't wait to profess your love; the future is not guaranteed.

Even though you can't read this chapter, Mom, *I love you*, and I always will.

Sonia Ventura is a former insurance agent and top boys' basketball coach. Currently, she is a department manager with Home Depot. Her love of teaching and coaching will eventually land her in the classroom. In particular, her ability to communicate across gender, cultural, and racial lines has uniquely qualified her to motivate and inspire underserved communities. Sonia currently holds a bachelors degree in education and is pursuing a masters degree in education.

She is proud of her Puerto Rican heritage and is affectionately known as Papi. You can follow

Sonia on Twitter @ atlantaspapi

Defying Convention

IS IT THE COLOR OF MY SKIN OR THE SCARF ON MY HEAD?

Asila Abdul-Haqq

When I think about being an African American, Muslim, and female in American society, I recall all of the struggles I have once faced and all the struggles that are yet to come. Knowing that I am a triple minority (or a triple threat to some) makes me think differently about the world and myself. It forces me and encourages me to become smarter. Media programming doesn't prioritize my life or thinking process; the haters don't faze me because I know I am above them. And the customary societally influenced social activities don't appeal to me either. Being a Black Muslim female in American society fuels what struggles I have faced pertaining to my racial, religious, and sexual description and how I have grown to conquer them.

As many of us know, the African American race has been oppressed as a minority for hundreds of years across the world. Slavery began with White American superiority, and through generations, even though racial discrimination and segregation have been outlawed, families have grown and reproduced with that same philosophy that Blacks are inferior and Whites are superior, which affects our everyday lives and the way we live with ourselves.

Every person I have been acquainted with knows to some extent exactly what I am talking about, even in the present day. For example, when I walk into a seminar or fundraiser in which the majority is White, or a race other than African American, the hospitality level in the room drops. Even now, I sometimes overhear the waiters arguing over who serves the table I am sitting at, and then one comes to my table and avoids eye contact with me and engages in the least amount of conversation possible. This type of discrimination is present in both public and private places. Still, it makes me wonder if it's the color of my skin or the scarf on my head.

Asila Abdul-Haqq

In the most popular and well-known media, Islam is targeted as a terrorist religion all over the world, but especially in the United States of America. Never is this more evident than in television news, which tells multiple stories of Islamic threats to the public's attention, perpetuating the idea that Islamic terrorism has caused many other religious groups to despise Islam and its efforts. Movies and television often shine a negative light on Muslims, which people think doesn't affect their opinions on Islam, but it does. They program the human brain to think a certain way, which in turn leads to more hatred of Islam in the public's heart.

The unfair media attention does discourage me and so many other Muslims, but it also gives us a purposeful reason to remain strong. We also know that we have to represent Islam with our actions and appearances, and prove the general media wrong; Muslims are peaceful and are not a threat to nonviolent civilization. Because I know that Muslims are negatively and violently targeted every day by different people in many ways, I walk around cautious of what I say and what I do. Just wearing a scarf on my head, called a hijab, immediately pronounces me as a Muslim woman, and because of media influences, this associates me with the words "violent" or "terrorist."

I know some may think that Muslim women purposely make themselves an easy target by wearing the hijab, and I partially agree, because as soon as anyone sees a woman with a scarf wrapped around her head, he or she immediately assumes she is a Muslim. However, one of the most important things I have learned over my short life is to love my hijab. Hijab, in the Arabic language, means "cover," and Muslim women associate it with modesty. Many Muslims live in fear or self-hatred and don't wear their hijab with the honor it deserves. Sometimes, they even hate it. But other Muslimahs (Muslim females) like me embrace it to the point where we couldn't take it off if our lives depended on it. When I put on my hijab, I feel gifted, as though I've been chosen to represent something amazing, and even though Islamic representation through hijab may lead to some negatives socially, it is worth it because it is what I believe in and what I believe I was made and born for.

When I was younger, I remember that most of my Muslim classmates and friends didn't wear their hijab outside of Islamic school, and their parents didn't force them to. Of course, I wondered why I had to wear mine, and I desired to expose my hair and arms and legs. As you may gather from this, a hijab is more than just a scarf; it is also a covering over your hair, arms, and legs. Additionally, it is a state of mind in which you save all of your physically attractive body parts for the eyes of your husband and your family. This alone makes me a female minority in society.

For centuries, both men and women have oppressed females. In the greatest stories and histories, women were sometimes captured as slaves or killed for the fun of murder, or they were subjugated for their so-called weak-mindedness, which gave men a sense of power and superiority. Even now, some men expect women to do what seen as a female's responsibility. Even in jest, tension is created between the two sexes because of a female's "inferiority." For example, I work at a camp that only allows women to work there, so it is an all-female staff. Of course, my co-workers and I have male friends who will come up to our job and ask if our camp has any job openings, and we reply no. But even if there were, they wouldn't qualify because of their gender. Then they will say, "You know guys work better than girls; you should just stay at home and do some chores or something." Normally, we laugh, but even this shows that males and females still haven't gotten over the outdated notion of female inferiority out of their minds, which is shown in everyday life. For this reason, women have to work harder to show that they have the same rights as workers as men.

After reading about being an African American, a Muslim, and a woman in American society, I believe the reader deserves to have a taste of the combination of all three: being an African American Muslim woman in America. In the past few years, learning who I am and who I want to be has been a major part of my personal and spiritual growth. When you know that every day that you walk outside your house – well, even before that, when I look at myself in the mirror and wrap my scarf around my head, put on my underwear, my long pants, and shirt – and step out my bedroom door, I know that there are people out there who will look at me that believe I am less than them. Knowing this, though, has helped me to grow. I have grown in ways that I never thought were possible because I learned how to love myself. Before family, before friends, and with God, I learned how to love myself and know that who I am, what I look like, and where I came from are all extraordinary parts of me that I should be willing to share with anyone and everyone I encounter.

I have so many stories for each and every characteristic of myself, as well as the way the public has responded to them. Most people my age don't talk like me, think like me, or dress like me. And as I mentioned before, being part of a triple minority group makes the naturally intelligent (which is all of us) even smarter, and people can see that. That is why some people out there are classified as haters. These haters can see what is different and unique about you, and because they can't live up to that, they become jealous and hate you for it. Knowing this helps you to accept who you are, and that is advice I give to you. You can't hate yourself and expect others not to hate you, too. When you love yourself, others become intrigued by your presence and begin to love you, too.

Last year was my first year at a new school, an Islamic school, but the dominant races were Desi and Arab. If they were considered Black, they were immigrants. Of course, at the beginning of the school year, because I was obviously African American, the administration and teachers put me in beginners' level classes, and I complained to each and every one of them until I was tested and put through intermediate and then to advanced. By the time I got to all advanced classes, which took about five days, all of the students and teachers in each level grew to envy me, and though I was aware of it, I didn't acknowledge it.

Being trilingual, I went to an advanced class that consisted only of native Arabs, including the teacher. The teacher and the students always excluded me from class activities, and would talk about me in front of my face in Arabic, as if I couldn't hear or understand them. They would make race and nationality-specific insults about me, and I would answer right back in Arabic. They would just mumble under their breaths about the "stupid Negro who thinks she knows everything." This shows that discrimination because of talents, color, or religion exists, even in the group you belong to, which is a sad truth about today's society.

When I was in the fifth grade, I remember recently skipping the fourth grade and encountering a new girl, built tough and thick, who acted tough and thick, and everyone wanted to be her friend because they knew not to mess with her. Of course, me being extremely young and naive, I had no idea who she was or that I should be afraid of her, so I minded my business and started fifth grade with straight A's and a smile on my face. About a month later, she threatened and cursed at me, and as time went by, the threats became worse. Soon, I was being bullied because of my intelligence, my age, and my physical beauty. Being so weak, I never asked anyone for help. I never tried to fight back and instead acted as if I was fine. But the treatment only got worse.

One day, I told my mother a tiny bit of what was going on in the classroom, until everything spilled out and I couldn't protect my bully anymore. My mother was thoroughly appalled. She had raised me to excel academically and hoped that doing so would make me strong during my rudimentary years and beyond. She talked to the vice principal, who was her friend, and after several months of fighting for justice against my bully, the girl was finally expelled.

If you are a mother reading this, you either know or are soon to know that your child will grow up to be strong only if he or she learns to stand back up after falling down, to fight his or her battles. Eventually, I learned that it's not always about winning the battles; it's about winning the war. Now, I'm not only talking about the war against bullies, or even racism, but the war within you. We all complain about our personal problems, about depression and instability, but sometimes you don't need to swim or jump out of the river. I've learned to ride with the current and float down my river so I can learn exactly what I need to succeed as an African American Muslim woman in America, and I advise you to do the same.

My name is **Asila Abdul-Haqq**, and I attend Al Falah Academy High School, and I intend to study gynecology and engineering in the near future.

MY GRANDPA'S POLITICS:
"WE'RE RAISING ADULTS NOT CHILDREN."

Di Neo

Politics. That thing everyone either talks about or totally hates to talk about. It's that big thing with which men pursue power and run countries. At least that's what we're told it is. Or maybe it's just the way us young people understand it. For people my age and younger, it's that totally uncool thing to talk about, never mind getting involved in.

Like many Black South Africans born during my time and before, I was born into a great family in a village. The remarkable part of my story is that for the first fourteen years of my life, I was raised by a man, my paternal grandfather. Now, I know what you're thinking: how did that happen? Well, it's a long story, perhaps one I'll share with you someday. But back to the story I'm telling now. Politics.

Being raised by a man, which wasn't – and still isn't – the norm, automatically made me different to other kids. But it also allowed me certain advantages, advantages that were not the norm for a girl. As u*mXhosakazi*, a *Xhosa* maiden, there are many things that our culture forbids girls and women from doing. I did many of these uncustomary things. I went to places and did things that other girl children never got to do. For example, while the women and girls worried about being around men at the kraal, I would often walk in with careless abandon. I have eaten every part of a sheep reserved for only boys and men. And when only the girls did their "girl" chores, like washing dishes and cleaning the house, I read books and newspapers. Because I was raised differently, I did all of this and more. So, of the many wonderful stories of my childhood, I'd like to share some with you.

I must have been eight or nine when it happened. A group of older men were sitting under a tree socializing and drinking *umqombothi*, a traditionally brewed African beer, talking about things that were affecting the village. I remember wearing my red dress. I tell you this because it's important. I don't want you to think that the men mistook me for a boy. I walked over because they seemed to be concentrating on each other's faces as they passed around the communal beer. Having been around men a lot, I knew that they were talking about something serious. My grandpa always had that look every time he read his court documents or books. So I walked over to them to try and help them figure out the problem. I didn't shyly stand within earshot as custom dictated a curious boy would do. I walked right up to them, greeted them, and asked how I could help them figure out what seemed to be bothering them. They looked at me with comedic amazement and laughed.

I know you have had this experience, too, where folks just don't take you seriously at first. Something about the person they've decided you are just doesn't impress them.

"You think you can fix problems?" one man asked me. "Yes," I replied boldly.

I was convinced that if I gave it my all, perhaps I could help them, and then I could brag to my grandpa about how I had helped fix a grown-up problem that day. So I was determined.

But one of the men that laughed told them who my grandfather was and then proceeded to humour me. I smiled and affirmed that he was correct about who my grandfather was and one of them asked me what I think must happen to stop the young men in the village who had developed a nasty habit of stealing chickens to sell for beer and cigarettes.

I remember thinking about the question. This was a complicated situation. There were two issues I knew were involved. Both those issues were passionate issues of discussion in my house, issues of legal and moral importance. I understood these concepts well. I looked at them for a while, thinking about whether I was giving the right answer.

"That depends," I said.

Surprised, they returned my gaze. I will never forget how I felt being looked at with real intent in their eyes. Being seen. Being considered.

"And what would it depend on?" one of them asked me with serious curiosity.

"On what you were prepared to do yourselves," I replied confidently with a smile. "And what would you have us do?" the same man asked.

"Well," I began, "you would have to decide how it is you wish the boys to learn the lessons. There are two lessons to learn. One is the legal lesson and the other is the moral lesson. The legal lesson is that if you tell the police, they'll take them to jail. But if you want to teach them a moral lesson, then you will have to be the moral standard."

I remember them looking at me like I had said something they had never heard before. I was really pleased with myself. And even though I had stolen this piece of advice from the countless conversations and lessons my grandpa and I had been involved with, I knew that they had not considered this line of thought, and I had therefore been of use. I had been listened to. I had been heard. I contributed. I mattered. Many times, they would call me to come and talk with them. Soon I had a reputation of being "the smart kid."

Years later, I would come to understand that I was heard that day because of a man, my grandpa. He acted as my signifier. Because of my affiliation with him, I had become someone who could be given "the light of day," as it were. If that one man hadn't known he had raised me, I never would have been listened to. I wouldn't have been heard. I wouldn't have contributed. I wouldn't have mattered. I would have been dismissed and told to go and wash the dishes or help my mother.

This principle is replicated in almost every situation in the lives of girls and women. Take something as ridiculous as the movies for instance. The leading actress' presence is always signified by her affiliation with the male. Of course, when parents give money to their children to go and watch "the biggest rom-com of the season," they don't think, "Let me send my daughter to a film that tells her that her significance is tied to how she fits into the man's idea of who she is, can be, or contributes." If that is what they thought, I imagine rom-coms in their current formats would be something of the past. In my own life, this principle has replicated itself many times. But because I was raised differently, I was able to deal with the discomfort without, perhaps, the political jargon to say, "I am feeling oppressed as a girl." So although I could never have fully comprehended the politics of not just patriarchy, but the socialization that designates children and adolescents as people not to be heard but merely seen, I affirmed, through my actions, what I had been taught, which was to demand something different.

Di Neo

In my grandfather's house, I was listened to. My opinion of things was sought. Every day I was asked to read and was asked questions about the texts. I watched the *Xhosa* news every evening and was asked questions about it. I got so good at watching the news that during the holidays we spent at Dabawo's (my aunt) house, I was the designated "news watcher." And when she came home from work late, I would relay everything I had heard.

One night she came home, and I told her the news as usual. But I made a mistake.

"Also, on the news, they said that the government is planning to undertake a big program to help '*abantu basetyhini*,'" I told her excitedly. "Isn't that great, Dabawo?" I said smiling up at her.

"Yes," she said. "That is great."

"Do you think we will be able to see the news people when they get there?" I asked, excited at the prospect of seeing the people who made TV news.

"Get where?" she asked me curiously.

"At Tyhini," I said. "You know, where Nelson Mandela lives. The government is going to help the people there, and the TV news people are going to come."

She burst out laughing. A roaring and long laughter. I loved her laughter. It had always been such a happy sound. I smiled at the sound of it, at the look on her face. When she finally composed herself, she looked at me and said, "Who told you that?"

"The news people," I said. I was unsure of myself now. I looked around at my siblings and cousins, wishing they could tell her I was right. But they paid no attention to the news and provided no help. So I looked back at my aunt.

"*Abantu basetyhini* means 'people who are female,'" she told me lovingly. I could see the smile still resting on the edges of her lips. "The government is going to help women. Mandela lives in Qunu."

"Aaaaah," I said, feeling stupid. How could I have gotten the two mixed up? I internally chastised myself and felt rather stupid. I had not heard that version of the word "women" in my mother tongue. I had indeed grown up differently. While the women taught girls and boys their gender words and roles, I was never preoccupied with gender. So non-existent was the preoccupation of gender in my home that I, at ten, didn't even know the word.

I knew only what I was told by my grandpa, which was that I was smart, capable, and, with application and diligence, would one day be able to resolve complicated legal and moral issues as Chief Justice of the highest court in the land, the Constitutional Court of South Africa. And although being male was an unspoken requirement then, and may still even be today, I was raised to believe otherwise.

Unfortunately, as with all of us, the first restrictors of our freedoms, the people that dim our light, are our kin. It was no different for me. I clearly remember the first time I became aware of politics. It was after my unknown brush with patriarchy and my lack of understanding of gender and institutionalized gender roles. I was maybe eleven years old. My dad used to make my brother, cousin, and I do karate because we were really big Bruce Lee fans, me being more of a fan than they were. If you are familiar with Bruce, you know he worked on getting his body strong, and so, naturally, I worked to look like him. I know what you are thinking: as a girl, I could never look like him. Well, you would be right. But

The Strength of My Soul

I really didn't know that then. Let's just say, I was smart in other ways, not so much about human biology.

So one afternoon, while doing our karate sparring, I proudly took off my shirt to show my dad that my chest was growing from the training I was doing. My aunt happened to be in the kitchen at that very moment and she had witnessed the whole thing. As my dad was congratulating me, my aunt flew into the living room.

"Put on your shirt," she commanded. "And don't you ever walk around without a shirt on again. Can't you see you are growing breasts?"

I was shocked and confused. I didn't understand, because I had believed that the chest was growing as a result of my training, like Bruce Lee. Anyway, I put my shirt back on and never took it off. So one day, during one of the school holidays we spent at my grandmother's house, I went to her.

"Grandma," I began cautiously, not sure how to ask, "why am I growing breasts?"

She didn't even look at me, since she was busy packing the stock onto the isle shelf. "Because you are a girl," she said simply.

I felt, from her response, that I should understand what that meant. But I did not. I was going to let go of the conversation, but the sinking feeling in my spirit wouldn't let me, so I braved another question.

"What things can boys do that girls can't?" My eleven-year-old self couldn't bear to look at her when I asked the question. I can't tell you why, except that somewhere in my gut I thought there was a lot, and I was afraid I was right. My grandmother stopped to look at me. She pulled my face to face her.

"Girls can do everything that boys can do," she said. "But they are not always allowed."

I have come to learn that this is true for many of us because politics isn't that big thing that happens when men become presidents and start wars or peacekeeping missions. By the time it gets to that point, those boys were raised in homes that said that they could be presidents. They were taught by teachers and professors who affirmed it. And they went to jobs where by age forty-five they could realistically vie for positions of president in their companies and countries.

Politics, you see, is the sum total of how you raise

your children. Freedom, fairness, and equality are not merely political campaign slogans; they are practised, or not, at home. Kids may not have the vocabulary for these concepts, but they are a daily reality of their experience. See, schools don't teach us these concepts. They only reveal whether we have experienced them or been robbed of them.

My grandpa's philosophy was to raise adults, not children. It's not a perfect philosophy, just different. The operative words there are the verb "raise" and the noun "adults." He did more than just tell me I was great and capable – he applied his teaching by creating the environment for me to be great and always expected it of me.

Raise your children with the expectation that no matter who they are and what they are, they will meet the world as equals to everyone. My home was not a perfect home; nobody's home is. My grandpa was not a perfect parent; nobody's parent is. He just raised me differently. Maybe it's because of his experience in life as a Black man. I don't know.

What I know for sure is that those of us who experience the least freedom, fairness, and equality at home soon come to experience the same in the world outside, because the personal is the political, and it doesn't get any more personal than one's home. Our homes cannot be the birthplaces we experience the –isms of the world in – racism, sexism, ageism, and other associated "freedom, fairness, and equality" snatchers like patriarchy, heteronormativity, etc.

Today, as a young African gay woman, I am most grateful to my grandpa for raising me differently.

Di Neo is a filmmaker, writer, and activist. She is founder of Kei Media, Africa's first LGBT- focused production company. She is creator and manager of the #ImYourAlly campaign, a LGBT project that seeks to create social cohesion around LGBT equality by creating and collaborating with ALLIES of all races, nationalities, religions, sexual orientations, etc. Di Neo is also a passionate feminist and a lover of books, people, art, food, and sport. She is currently working on finishing her first novel and feature screenplay. She believes in collaboration to lift the impact and reach of bodies of work. You can follow her work here:

Kei Media www.facebook.com/KeiMedia
@KeiMediaOrg
#ImYourAlly Campaign

www.facebook.com/pages/Im-Your-Ally-Campaign/863331383704095

MY UNFINISHED CHAPTER

Nijole Beth

Whenever I'm locked in a confined space, I pace and think of random things to keep sane, to avoid dwelling on the situation at hand. Is there a TV to watch, a book to read, a round object to toss? The pathetic artifacts of this inmate's life remind me of objects that were once everything to me: a stack of books, a handmade chessboard, a few scattered pieces of artwork taped to the concrete, a family photo, and large manila envelopes full of letters.

What I want to tell the world is that no part of my experience – not the uncertainty of when I would be free again, not the tortured screams of other prisoners – was worse than the three years I spent in solitary confinement. What would they say if I told them I needed human contact so badly that I woke every morning hoping to be interrogated? Would they believe that I once yearned to be sat down in a padded, soundproof room, blindfolded and questioned just to talk to somebody? How do you compare, when the difference between one person's stability and another's insanity is found in tiny details? Do I point out that I had a mattress, while they have thin pieces of foam, or that where I was imprisoned, the inmates have to shit at the front of the cell, in view of the guards? Human beings are social creatures. We are social not just in the trivial sense that we like company, and not just in the obvious sense that we each depend on others. We are social in a more elemental way: simply to exist as a normal human being requires interaction with other people.

I'm often asked what it was like being there, and that is a hard question to answer. This is because your circumstances change over the years. There is also no common ground to start from, nothing to compare it to. My standard answer is, "Imagine being locked behind two steel doors into a very small bathroom, and three times a day, large, angry men bring food to you. Five times a week, three of those large, angry men chain you up and escort you with sticks to a slightly larger room for an hour of court-mandated recreation." That's an incomplete answer, but it usually ends the conversation, which is the point.

I was actually almost three years into my sentence when I was locked up in the special housing unit under investigation for a possible violation of the rules. Eventually, I was cleared, but it was an unpleasant few months no less. Those aspects and others, like the fact that the only view from my window was steel girders, concrete walls, razor wire, and a thin sliver of the sky, had to have an effect on me. But what? I'm not comfortable in crowds, but then again, I never really was. But am I more hyper alert than I would be had I just been in general population? Would I have been any more of a light sleeper or an insomniac? I don't know. But when I compare myself with some of the ladies I was incarcerated with, I wonder why some of us are semi-normal or semi-okay, and some are very much neither.

My name is _____.

Much of the time, people develop the wrong impression of what happens on the other side of those barbed wires and what happens leading up to it. With that being said, I am going to share some of what happened in my life that led up to my incarceration. This is my story.

I just wanted to get quick money, but I found out early that no money is that easy. First of all, stripping can be bad on the psyche. You analyze your body down to the tiniest flaw, finding fault with everything. You go from feeling good – men are paying a lot of money to see you dance – to feeling like a used hand rag.

I stayed high a lot.

I needed to survive being on my own. I needed money because there was so much pressure to have access to money, the perfect body, and the right lifestyle. At fifteen, I lived on my own in Miami. I had an apartment, a new model car, access to the drug of my choice, a man, a woman, and most importantly, a job. I learned to be self-sufficient and to become the financial provider in my relationships.

When I realized that I had an attraction to females, I did what I thought was the right thing at the time – I expressed it to my mother. I never grew up with her, and being in a new place, in a new country, I thought we could finally have the type of open relationship I had seen on television. The type of relationship in which I could tell her anything and she would love me no matter what. But reality came swiftly. Oh, she loved me enough.

That was evident. However, she told her husband at the time about my revelation, and he wasn't too keen on having a lesbian in his home. It was during one of their epic fights that I had the grand thought of defending my mother against this man. He was already hyped from their arguing when he said those infamous words to me: "I don't want no lesbian dyke bitch living in dis house."

I looked to my mother, because surely she would defend me; she would support me. He can't kick me out! I'm her daughter. I am the baby at that. He knew he messed up. At least that's what I thought.

I was stunned. My mother agreed with her husband. It was comical to me that not even thirty seconds ago, they were about to tear each other's throats out, but as soon as I tried to intervene, they became a united front in kicking me out of the only house I really knew at the time. I didn't cry, I laughed. I laughed so hard, I cried.

Needless to say, I threw all my belongings in a black, Hefty garbage bag and set off down the street. Just me and Mr. Hefty. I remember thinking that maybe it was just to get him to calm down. I thought she was going to realize that he was wrong to put her fourteen-year-old daughter on the street with nothing but a garbage bag of clothes and come get me. Maybe she needed to calm down as well. I thought I would give her that time, so I waited. And waited. And waited some more. I remember sleeping behind the Publix Supermarket next to the door so that if someone were to come out, I would be hiding between the door and the ramp. I waited and waited, but my mother never came.

At fourteen years old, I did my best to resume some degree of normalcy; I had no other choice. I slept outside at night, went to Cumberland Farms gas stations in the morning to clean up, and then went to school. My girlfriend at the time offered me a place to stay with her and her family, and I accepted. I was grateful. But I was still determined to make a life of my own. It almost became an obsession to prove to my family that they were wrong for kicking me out. I wanted to show that I was valuable – that I had worth.

I turned to dancing to make quick money. I didn't think I was doing anything wrong. I was just making a living. Of course, there is no way to make "quick money"; there's always a struggle. I liked dancing enough. No, that's not true. I *loved* it. I felt powerful being onstage; I didn't care about anything. At the time, I was taking ecstasy to take the nervousness away. And I kept in the forefront of my mind that I needed the money. I was *not* going to fail. As long as the money was there, I tantalized and tempted the men, and sometimes women. Yes, I entertained both men and women, and even though there is a stereotype about men being the aggressors, at times, to be honest, women were just as, if not more, aggressive. I said yes when they requested a private dance. The money was my allure. Anything for a dollar!

At times I felt powerful. Other days, I really didn't feel like doing anything. And still other days, I was so drained from school that I was grateful I didn't have to be onstage. But I had dreams. Make money, enroll in college, find a husband, perhaps put a down payment on a house – isn't that all part of the American dream? God bless America.

I met my boyfriend, Eddie, in the club. Cliché, I know. My girlfriend was one of Eddie's best customers for his rural pharmaceutical entrepreneurship. I hope you understand what that is. Eddie and I were friends of sorts, but eventually we became more. He was my mentor, my savior, and my guru, if you will. To me he wasn't just a rag tag, around-the-way guy. No, Eddie had power, connections, and class. He was who I needed to be. He taught me how to be a lady, how to walk, talk, dress, eat – everything. We took trips and stayed in places I never thought I would stay. It was a great lifestyle. But, being with Eddie had consequences; the tradeoff just wasn't worth it.

Yes, in public, we were perfect. I smiled and deferred to him. I treated him and catered to him like a king. However behind closed doors, he treated me like I was the pill-popping stripper I felt I was. If I had spoken out of turn to one of his friends, he would beat me. If I had chosen the wrong fork to eat, he would beat me. I was tired of him making *all* the decisions for me, even down to my underwear. It wasn't just the physical beatings, though; eventually those faded. It was the psychological beatings that still have an adverse effect on me.

Eddie asked for my hand in marriage. I was afraid and declined. I knew I didn't love him; I feared him. At the same time, I was loyal to my girlfriend and what she was going through. But I wasn't in love with her either. She had become an addict, and I didn't want to leave her in the state she was in. How could I? That would have been heartless. Even for me.

Eddie didn't take the rejection too well. We literally fought for days. In the end, though, I was the one who was at fault. I was the one who had tried to kill him. I was the one who went ballistic and tried to take a life.

Soon, I was in jail, waiting for yet another continuance, when my attorney suggested I have a psychological evaluation. This would at least put on record that I was not in my right state of mind when I had committed my crime. They're kidding right? I didn't need an evaluation. I was fine. I was just a teenager living on her own without any support and guidance. I was tired of fighting, I was tired of the beatings, and I was tired of being scared. Sure, I might've gone overboard in my actions, but who really stops to think of the consequences *before* they happen?

Right? Right?

I submitted to two tests: the Minnesota Multiple Personality Inventory, or the MMPI for short, and a Kevlar test with 567 questions. I had three different psychologists from the prosecution's side interview me. They asked seemingly weird and random questions. Yet I understood why. To hear the results of my testing and interviews, I had to go to a competency hearing. Based on the results, I was diagnosed as paranoid schizophrenic with bipolar disorder and battered women's syndrome. Say that ten times fast.

I truly did not understand what any of that meant. It's like they were speaking an alien language around me. When it was all said and done, I was remanded to undergo mental health treatment at the South Florida Evaluation and Treatment Center. I was ordered to take any and all medications the doctors deemed necessary, and to be there as long as the doctors deemed necessary. I didn't stay that long; I left after thirty-three days and was remanded into custody until my trial.

After all that I had gone through, I was sentenced collectively to eighteen years in the state penitentiary, followed by fifteen years on probation. I didn't know how to react to that. My mother was devastated. My girlfriend was hysterical. I was numb. But I was more at peace because at least I knew the outcome, the verdict. It was now time for me to adjust to my new life. My life. As prisoner L45250.

Nijole Beth

I lived with murderers, thieves, rapists, extortionists – the so-called "dregs" of society. My first month, I didn't speak to anyone. I just did what I was told. Not out of fear, but because I was adjusting to life inside prison.

There was a hierarchy that I wasn't aware of until I was actually in a "family." And that happened quite by accident. I was involved in a brawl in the kitchen I was assigned to work at. It really was a melee. The officers couldn't tell who started the fight, so they arrested all eleven of us; the inmates who were involved in the fight initially tried to "investigate." The trouble was that no one knew how the fight had initially started, except for me. I had witnessed it all. I saw when the two women decided to conduct their "business," what we knew on the inside was illegal activities, close to where I was. I guess the deal did not go as planned, and so there was war.

The end result? Seven inmates were let go because they all said I had seen everything. I ended up going to confinement with the two studs and one girl. And still I didn't say anything. The older stud had asked me why I didn't say anything to get out of confinement, and I told her it wasn't my place to help the officers. From then on I was her adopted "son."

Initially, I played into the whole prison scenario. To be called the most respected inmate's "son" had a lot of perks. In some aspects, I was young, and dumb. I went to confinement more often. Not because I did anything, but I was always under investigation. I had a reputation for not speaking about anything that I saw. I went to confinement so many times that the sergeants, captains, and lieutenants all had my mother's number on hand.

I played into being a prisoner. For a long time, I didn't even like myself. I even tried to commit suicide while I was there. I just knew I couldn't be in prison anymore, and I wanted my life to end. After my initial suicide attempt, I became a cutter. I self-mutilated, not for attention but because I wanted to have some type of feeling to let me know that I wasn't just a drone. I hated myself.

About two years before I left prison, I realized that I was tired. I was tired of people, I was tired of the system, and I was tired of being tired. It took me a while to find peace within, but eventually I found it through meditating. I really prayed, wholeheartedly. I created goals. I had a "vision album." You know, similar to a vision board but with an album. I still have it. The vision album contained everything I was looking forward to doing and having after I left the penitentiary. I made the conscious decision that no matter what, I was going to be different. Better. Accepting.

I have learned that accepting yourself and not letting society's labels (i.e. criminal, convict, evil, etc.) define you can make all the difference in your life. And honestly, it is very difficult at first to not take some of the labels to heart. But I have learned, and I want you to know, that you are so much more than the disparaging labels society places on you. It took me quite a while to understand and accept that, but I know that now. And I want you to know that, too.

Yes, maybe at one point you were incarcerated, or still are, but that is not *all* that you are. Loving myself despite everything has helped me rise above and realize that I am more than what society thinks I am. Now is the time to prove everyone wrong. Now is the time to show society that I am not just a "criminal." I am a contributing and vital member of society. Now is the time to love myself. And now is the time for you to love yourself.

Remember that every saint has a past, and every sinner has a future. Self-acceptance is a process, and it does take some time. You will be better off once you learn that you cannot change everything about yourself, and you can't change your past. And that's okay. I am not perfect and I am never going to be. Fortunately, God does not expect perfection.

I was incarcerated for a total of fifteen years. Thankfully, I was released in 2013 on Mother's Day. Thankfully, I am successfully rebuilding my life. I have friends who love me and believe in me. Most importantly, I love and believe in myself.

Nijole Beth is working on her memoir and looks forward to empowering women to love themselves and to accept themselves.

LIVE LIFE ON YOUR OWN TERMS

Sheena Yap Chan

I only have one request: have the *courage* to live life on your own terms. Do what makes you *happy*, because you deserve to live a better life.

I was born and raised in the Philippines and come from a very large Asian family. Being an Asian woman from such a large Asian family, and I mean *large*, women are supposed to act a "certain" way. We are expected to follow all the rules, made by men of course. Rules like when an Asian woman gets married, she is expected to leave her family and live with her husband in his hometown, where the wife is subordinate to the whims of her mother-in-law. And If any woman goes against the rules, she is considered "out of control," disobedient, wild, and crazy.

The Strength of My Soul

In a traditional Asian family, men were always superior and women were inferior. We had to toe the line and accept the decisions that were laid out for us, because if a woman did something that was considered socially unacceptable, people would gossip like there's no tomorrow. Your family name could also get damaged along the way. Just one little mistake could result in "toxic talk" that would circulate for months. This talk wasn't just limited to your own extended families, either. The conversations from outside of the family could ruin a woman's life, personally and professionally.

Because of how most Asian women are taught to act, and because of the repercussions of doing anything contrary to those teachings, most Asian women behave according to tradition and culture. As a result, society sees us as submissive, and this stereotype has kept me stuck in a life that was literally choking me. In general, this stereotype damages a woman's self-esteem and limits her life. Still, I always knew I wanted more than a stereotypical life. Even today, most Asian women have never had a say in their own lives because their parents or other relatives dictated them. My own grandmother was a perfect example. She was forced into a marriage that she did not want. But because she believed it was her duty as a daughter to obey her father's rules, she married a man she didn't love.

This is somewhat true for me as well. Since most Asian women are conditioned by their culture to live a dependent life, I was told what to do and when to do it for most of my life. I was told to go to school, get good grades, go to the university, get a job, get married, have kids, be the good and dutiful wife, and never rock the boat. I had to play the role of the good daughter, the good sister, the good granddaughter, and so on. I was the obedient child who pleased my family and my relatives so that our "name" would never be tarnished in public. Still, I knew I wanted something more than just the life that was set out for me. I knew there was more to life than just going along with what others wanted me to do. I wanted to have my own business, to be a motivational speaker, to travel the world, and more.

Perhaps you also have dreams and goals that you have been yearning to fulfill but are scared of what your family or your culture may think or say. For example, I always knew that I wanted to work for myself. There was a part of me knew that there was more to life than working in a cubicle. Over the years, there were many times I wanted to quit my job and branch out on my own to become my own boss. But my parents told me that it was "too scary" to become an entrepreneur. They wanted me to have that "security" in a job. And because I didn't want to worry them, I decided to stay in my job even though I was not happy. In trying to please them, I always played it safe and never really fully lived my life. And what did playing it safe ever do for me?

Well, let me tell you. Even as an adult, I was never confident in making my own decisions, because I always needed the approval of others. One time, I wanted to find another job because I wanted a higher salary. When I asked my coworker if I was doing the right thing, he answered, "No, because you are a woman and the money you make now is more than enough for a woman." So I never pursued any other job and stayed in my office job for twelve *long* years. I let my coworker make me believe that I couldn't get a better job with better pay. I believed him more than I believed myself.

The truth is, I was too afraid to take any meaningful risks in my life. As a result, I found myself working in a cubicle for the same company for twelve years. I was not fulfilled. Further, working there made me feel like I was dying inside.

Although I was grateful to have the job, I felt like a zombie going into the office day in and day out. For twelve long years (3,120 days), I felt numb, as if life was passing me by. Have you ever felt as if you were living on the outside, but slowly dying on the inside?

Overall, I never trusted myself, which meant I never pursued anything in life worth *risking*! Do you ever feel that way? Do you ever feel like you don't trust yourself because you fear making bad choices in life? If so, don't worry because I was the same way. I remember buying a car when I was twenty-seven because it was time for an upgrade. Now, I'm no expert about cars, but I knew I wanted to buy a particular car because of how I felt when I drove it. I loved driving it. It rode so smoothly on the road. I knew it was for me. As soon as I finished test-driving the car, I told the salesman that I was going to buy it. It was the first time in my life I made a decision without asking for my parents' approval. A couple of nights after purchasing my car, I went to my parents' home to proudly show it off. However, when my father saw the car, he was upset.

You see, my father loves anything and everything to do with cars. So, when he found out I bought a car and didn't include him in the buying process, he was not a happy camper. He went outside and checked everything in the car to see if there were any defects that I had overlooked. As it turned out there were many defects. The miles on the car were too high, a small chip on the front window, and the paint was scratched. Even as an adult, I got in trouble for not including my parents in my decision to buy a car.

After my car purchase, I lost some confidence, because I thought I wasn't good enough to make the right decisions in my life. I felt as if I needed to ask my parents first before making any majors decisions. I didn't trust myself. But my boyfriend at the time told me something that I will never forget, something I want to pass on to you. He told me that even though buying the car wasn't the best decision on my part, I made the decision all by myself. His perspective really made me feel better about myself and about my decision. It may not seem big, but it was a big realization for me at that time. Instead of looking at the negative side of the situation, my boyfriend helped me to see what good had come out of it. He made me realize that if I could make one decision by myself and not feel bad about it, I could make another one, too.

After I made a decision to purchase the car, I started to make more decisions for myself. And while my family at first was opposed them, they understood that I was an adult, and that they had to let their little girl grow. They understood that I had to be responsible for my choices and my own life.

Now, I am not telling you to not listen to anything your parents say. My parents are the greatest parents I could ever ask for, and I am grateful for them every single day. However, there's a point in your life when *you* have to make the choices in your life regardless of what anyone tells you. You have to make yourself happy first.

I finally decided to live life on my own terms when my aunt passed away from a horrific accident in 2011. My aunt really knew how to fully live life. She was always willing to do things that most people in their late fifties would never do, like rock climbing, zip lining, and scuba diving. Even though people told her she was too old to do those things, she did them anyway because they made her happy.

But in 2011, she passed away. While on a hiking trip, she fell from a thirty-foot cliff and died. I still remember that day like it was yesterday. My sister called me in the most frantic voice, telling me my aunt passed away. Initially, I thought she was joking because I was in total shock that something like that could happen in real life. I thought events like that only happened in the movies.

Even now when I see her photo, I can't help but cry because I miss her. But then I remember that she was able to live her life according to her terms. Her life was more meaningful because of her adventures and because of the many people she inspired to live life to the fullest. That was when I knew I wanted things to change, and when I knew that things in my life had to change. Even though I had no clue then about what I would do, I knew I had to do something differently. I still had that burning desire to branch out and become my own boss, and I knew that *now* was the time. I knew that I had to make changes or else I would feel like a zombie just walking around aimlessly in life.

I knew deep inside that I was meant for greater things. I knew that I wanted to be my own boss. So I made a decision to just go out and live my life no matter what people would say. I know how scary it can be, especially when there are so many people telling you you're crazy, wondering why you would do that when you're already successful and have a great job.

It was difficult, but I did it anyway. And to be honest, it was the best decision of my life. I was finally able to live one of my biggest dreams, which was to live in Hawaii for six months during the winter season. I followed my heart. Just think, because most people are married to their jobs or are too scared of what other think of them, they can't just pick up their things and live on a tropical island for six months.

I wouldn't have been able to live in Hawaii and pursue my dreams if I had followed what everyone else wanted me to do. I had to break with my tradition and trust myself, even if it meant doing what scared me the most, like putting up a video of myself on YouTube. Now I get to share my stories with you in this amazing book, with other amazing women sharing their stories to uplift you.

The biggest lesson that I learned is that if you want change, it has to start with *you!* You can't expect to inspire others if you can't even inspire yourself to do something out of your norm, culture, or tradition. Yes, it's scary, and yes, some people who are dear to you may tell you that you're crazy or that you are not supposed to do what you want. But, if you have this burning desire to do something that you have always wanted to do, go out there and do it. You deserve to live life to the fullest, on your own terms; you just have to go out there and get it.

People always say freedom is expensive, and it is. That is why only extraordinary people will do whatever it takes to get it. I know that you reading this is already a sign that you are an extraordinary person. You just needed the extra push to take the required action to do what you have always wanted to. I want to remind you to believe in yourself. Do what you deserve in life. And there's no better day to start than today! Go out there and live life on your own terms!

Be happy!

Sheena Yap Chan is a blogger and speaker whose sole purpose, drive, and passion is to help women live a better life through entrepreneurship. She continues to inspire women through her blog by providing marketing, social media tips, and advice to help women remove whatever keeps them from greatness. Currently, she is doing a 365-day blogging challenge, which means she is blogging every single day for one whole year. She also has a podcast that helps women build up their self-confidence. It's called The Tao of Self Confidence.

Always remember....
"Behind every successful woman is herself."

You can connect with Sheena via...

Podcast: www.thetaoofselfconfidence.com
Blog: www.sheenayapchan.com

Facebook Profile:
www.facebook.com/sheena.y.chan

Facebook Page:
www.facebook.com/sheenayapchan

Twitter & Instagram
@crasianpreneur

LIVING YOUR DREAMS WITH PURPOSE AND PASSION

Kim J. King

My story is designed to be the catalyst that leads you to closely examine your life and ensure that it aligns with your purpose. Living your life in harmony with your God-given purpose results in a rich, rewarding, and satisfying life. In other words, you can live out your dreams.

Shockingly, when I ask most people if they are living their dreams, they emphatically tell me no. Usually, I follow up by asking, "Why in the world do people choose not to live their dreams?" While the answers vary greatly, the reasons all seem to boil down to one simple truth: many people do not believe that it is possible to live their dreams.

In fact, many people believe that the concept of "living your dreams" is a fairy tale rooted in childish, naïve gibberish, having no validity in the "real world." Many authors have touted the theory that people should do what they love and the money will follow. In stark contrast, the paradigm that our society subscribes to is this: do what makes you the most money, given your education and experience, and do what you love on the weekend. Hence, Thank God Its Friday, or TGIF, is the unifying chant that most of the workforce understands and recites near the end of each work week. The "living your dreams" notion eludes the vast majority of the workforce.

The late, great Langston Hughes urged people to live their dreams in his poem entitled, *Dreams*. He warned of the gravity of failing to live our dreams by comparing the condition to a "broken-winged bird" and a "barren field frozen with snow." In essence, not living our dreams is a sad plight and a dismal existence! Are there people who dare to be different and follow their dreams no matter what? Yes! And this is where my story begins.

My parents raised me with all kinds of restrictions, which they thought would make me a good person. Many things that my friends could do, such as going to parties, attending prom, playing organized sports, and having boyfriends, were definitively off limits for me during the first eighteen years of my life. Many times I felt as if I were missing out on the fun my friends were experiencing. During these times, I was saddened, but I would quickly find things to do, think about, and act out to satisfy my mind, body, and spirit. Unbeknownst to me, I was in a dream incubator and was given multiple opportunities to practice hatching my dreams.

For example, I might imagine myself winning an Olympic event, winning first place as a woman jockey on a not-so-well-known horse, being a super hero and saving people from all kinds of problems, successfully performing the same stunts as Evil Knievel, and an infinite number of other grand things. I always thought and dreamed *big*, even though I didn't share many of my dreams with others.

In spite of my restricted life, my parents always suggested that I could be *anything* I wanted to be. Additionally, they never acted surprised by the few grandiose ideas that I shared with them. They listened and played along with me. Except I wasn't playing. I was always very serious about my ideas. After many years passed, my parents began to realize that I was serious about each and every idea I would broach with them. And at no time did either of my parents rain or douse water on my ideas. They were always very proud of all of my ideas (no matter how great or minuscule, no matter how pragmatic or far-fetched). They were supportive!

I now realize that this was an important foundational building block in my life. I had a built-in idea/dream support system. Many people are not fortunate enough to have anyone in their inner circle who supports their ideas and dreams. Whether you are five years old or seventy-five years young, a support system is necessary for the ongoing attainment of your dreams. If you don't have an idea/dream support system, you must build one in order to live your dreams. Fortunately, you can build one from external resources.

First, identify your areas of interest, namely, your life's purpose. This step can be the most difficult and daunting task for some because many have been distracted from their purposes for so long. If that is the case with you, you may require assistance in identifying and realizing your purpose and passion. Knowing your purpose is akin to knowing yourself. Once you know your life's purpose, you are ready to move to the next step.

Second, go to the library, bookstore, or online to obtain more information about your areas of interest. Read industry publications, join industry organizations, groups, and clubs, and subscribe to industry magazines and newspapers. Your mission is to learn as much as you can about your interest. This step will be a breeze for you because you are legitimately interested in the subject matter. You'll find that your thirst for knowledge will be like a refreshing drink of water on the hottest, liquid-depleting day you can recall. After all, you are learning more about *you*!

Third, connect with authors of books or resource materials, local meet-up groups, social media groups that share your interests, subject matter gurus, and any other entrepreneurs who are passionate about the subject matter. Allow these people to mentor you, encourage you, connect you, motivate you, and help you. In turn, provide as much service as possible to them to make the exchange reciprocal and balanced. In this way, no one will feel taken for granted, and everyone will want to assist each other.

And fourth, don't count all of your real friends out. Just because your friends have not supported your dreams does not mean that they will refuse to support you with the proper coaching. I believe in the adage "if they know better, they will do better." So, tell them how to be your friend and the type of support that you will need to begin living your dreams. Who knows, you could be the inspiration they need to begin living their dreams.

Settling was never an option for me. It was all or nothing. Either I was 100 percent involved and engaged, or I was not. I was never lukewarm. I prided myself on being authentic and not hypocritical. I determined whether I was in or out by how I felt about the activity, event, or situation. I applied this process to every aspect of my life, including my professional life. I never chased dollars, only dreams.

Since I was eighteen, one of my goals was to retire at thirty-five. I communicated my plan to my friends and anyone else who cared to indulge me in dream-based conversation. Many would laugh and change the subject, but I never joined in the laughter because I was quite serious about my plan. To me, life was much more than working an unfulfilling nine-to-five job. This did not mean I was without great jobs and well-respected positions for which I assumed responsibility. I did! It was just that I knew from an early age I was destined for greatness and had a special purpose that would positively affect the world. I felt as if my purpose-driven work could not be contained in one company, organization, or firm.

That probably explains why I would easily decide to leave a position or organization if I didn't feel challenged or grew bored. Furthermore, the amount of money was never a determining factor for me. I have numerous examples of leaving "good jobs" to seek more meaningful opportunities, growth, enrichment, and greater challenges, or to avoid managerial insecurities (aka plain stupidity).

I was never afraid that I would not obtain a better opportunity or that I would not be able to financially support myself. I knew I had never been without adequate provisions and God would continue to support me no matter what. Moreover, I knew that all of these experiences, interactions with others, and lessons were positioning me for my great purpose-driven work. For me, new opportunities meant excitement. And I couldn't wait to see what was around the corner.

Well, I ended up retiring two years earlier than

planned, at thirty years old. My carefree life consisted of writing, reading, traveling, training, and whatever else I felt like doing, whenever I felt like doing it. A couple of years later, I decided I wanted to own a law firm. So, I bought an established firm and built and expanded the practice to be of greater service to people. As you can see, living my dreams required me to take many twists and turns along the way, but I embraced the ride and enjoyed the journey.

For many, having the courage to leave your comfort zone is a tough proposition. It doesn't help that society does not readily support that behavior. People who dare to live their dreams no matter what are said to be flighty, irresponsible, immature, and out of touch with reality. Those are not words of aspiration, admiration, or affirmation. Who wants to wear that kind of label? The result is that most people travel down the road most traveled and make as much money as possible, forfeiting the opportunity to live their dreams. Most people choose to chase dollars instead of their dreams. It's almost like a person with an incurable and painful health condition. This person tolerates the pain by finding methods to make her as comfortable as possible. (Do note, however, that there is a distinct difference between having an incurable health condition and giving up on your dreams. The difference in summed up in the word: *choice*.)

Subscribing to society's paradigm and negative peer pressure is a choice, not an immutable condition. Therefore, many choose to accept less than rich, rewarding, and satisfying lives because they have been mentally conditioned to believe that living their dreams is impossible. Their social networks, consisting of their family, friends, work mates, and colleagues, help to reinforce the idea that what they are doing is "just the way it should be done," and is a necessary part of this thing we call life. What a dreadful perspective! Such an attitude coincides with the saying displayed on bumper stickers and t-shirts, which says, "Life's a _____, makes death more rewarding than life." And to think that most people's lives are predicated upon this paradigm. What a horribly sad thought.

The premise of my story is to challenge and undermine this societal paradigm as the greatest untruth and travesty ever told that victimizes, cripples, and destroys millions of lives. It takes more lives than every war in the history of mankind. Moreover, it is more debilitating because it has a strong support system that seeps into our homes, making it difficult to successfully fight. In spite of the high toll, many have successfully chosen to live their lives with passion in harmony with their natural talents and abilities, so they can have rich, rewarding, and satisfying lives. I am proud to be part of that select number, living my dreams according to how I was created. I am clear about my purpose and passion, and it is this: to help people turn their dreams into reality and their reality into wealth. Similarly, my passion is to help others identify and realize their natural talents and abilities and help them utilize them to achieve greatness.

Even though I was always determined to live my dreams, I wasn't always clear about the specifics. In fact, over the years, I developed numerous ideas was excited about each and every one. Not only that, I worked on each idea with some success. As I worked on these ideas, I began to refine and fine-tune my purpose and passion. Interestingly, in reflecting on my lengthy list of ideas, I realized that they were all in the same vicinity of my true purpose and passion. So, my efforts were not in vain.

I believe that we inherently know our life's purpose. The longer people are away from living in their purpose and passion, they may need to be reminded of who they are and what their great purpose is. Some people's dreams need to be resuscitated. That makes sense to me because dreams are life. When we stop dreaming, we stop living.

My belief system is unwavering and coincides with my hope that all men and women follow the great Architect's purpose for their lives. In that way, I believe we can experience real freedom. Freedom from living paycheck to paycheck. Freedom from the material and financial anxieties of the world. Freedom to expand, grow, and develop according to the desires of our heart. Freedom to be happy and content. Freedom to believe in spite of everything. Freedom to live our dreams without excuses. And, the freedom to live the great life that we were all uniquely designed to live.

I have always believed that I could do anything I desired. And I believe you can, too. I realize that I have very strong beliefs about the significance of living your life with passion and living your dreams.

I believe that you can only be happy if you are living your dreams.

I believe that you can only fully experience the richness of life if you are living your dreams. I believe that living your dreams is the solution to your problems.

I believe that the world would be a far better place to live if more people were living their dreams.

I believe that unemployment numbers would plummet if people were living their dreams.

I believe that companies would be far more profitable if they hired people who were living their dreams.

I believe our country's deficit could be re-birthed to health if we live our dreams. I believe that having the ability to live your dreams is a great gift from God.

I believe it absolutely warms God's heart when we use our natural talents and abilities to live and help others.

I believe that when people live their dreams, they receive extraordinary assistance and rewards from God.

I believe that the fear of living one's dreams is not from God.

The Strength of My Soul

I believe that living your dreams is not everything – it's the *only* thing that matters!

Do you share these beliefs? If you would like to be counted in the growing numbers of those taking a bold stand for themselves, I invite you to join the ranks and start living your dreams. Restore the excitement and zest for living your life that was specially designed for you. Courageously and proudly walk in your purpose and passion to give your life real meaning. You are worth it!

Live your dreams!

Kim J. King is the Managing Partner for the law firm of Kim J. King Associates, LLC, founded in 1999. The firm handles traditional practice areas of the law, such as business law, contract law, personal injury, bankruptcy, immigration, criminal, family, and real estate law, just to name a few. Ms. King has considerable expertise in matters relating to business expansion, investment, and the acquisition of commercial and residential real estate. However, Ms. King is most noted for retooling businesses and helping individuals develop winning ideas that propel them to the next level.

Kim J. King

Ms. King pursued her undergraduate studies and graduated magna cum laude from the University of Cincinnati. She earned her Juris Doctorate degree at Salmon P. Chase College of Law. Ms. King has held several impactful professional positions as in-house counsel for major corporations. But she is most proud of her service and contribution to the non-profit sector as the Managing Director of INROADS/Greater Cincinnati-Dayton and as general counsel for Wilberforce University. Both positions afforded her the opportunity to make a difference.

Ms. King continues to hold true to her passion by helping people pursue and realize their dreams so they can achieve their greatness. In addition to being a practicing attorney, Ms. King is a purpose and passion coach, an author, a master trainer, a motivational speaker, and an "edutainment" director with a genuine interest and love for developing people. She is the also the author of *The Universal Guide to Financial Abundance.*

Often described as dynamic, cooperative, and congenial, Ms. King is a quality individual who gets the job done. Striving for excellence is one of her goals. To her, the ultimate measure of success is to make a positive impact on each and every life she touches.

The Strength of My Soul

You can learn more about Ms. King at www.livingyourdreamswithkimjking.com and www.kimjking.com.

WE WANT TO HEAR FROM YOU!!!

If this book has made a difference in your life SharRon would be delighted to hear about it.
Leave a review on Amazon.com!

BOOK SHARRON TO SPEAK AT YOUR NEXT EVENT!

Send an email to:
SharRon@SharRonJamison.com

Learn more about SharRon at:
www.SharRonJamison.com

FOLLOW SHARRON ON SOCIAL MEDIA

 SharRon-Jamison   SharRonJamison

ntent.com/pod-product-compliance
LLC

.0B/915